GUIDEBOOK TO PLANNING
Strategic Planning and Budgeting Basics for the Growing Firm

Robert M. Donnelly

An Inc./Van Nostrand Reinhold Publication

VAN NOSTRAND REINHOLD COMPANY

Published by Van Nostrand Reinhold Publishing
135 West 50th Street, New York, N.Y. 10020

Van Nostrand Reinhold
480 Latrobe Street
Melbourne, Victoria 3000, Australia

Van Nostrand Reinhold Company Limited
Molly Millars Lane
Wokingham, Berkshire, England

Macmillan of Canada
Division of Gage Publishing Limited
164 Commander Boulevard
Agincourt, Ontario M1S 3C7, Canada

15 14 13 12 11 10 9 8 7 6 5 4 3 2 1

Library of Congress Cataloging in Publication Data

Donnelly, Robert M.
    Guidebook to planning.

    "An Inc./Van Nostrand Reinhold publication."
    Includes index.
    1. Corporate planning.   2. Budget in business.
I. Title.
HD30.28.D66   1984   658.4'012   84-3667
ISBN 0-442-22256-4

*To all managers everywhere who know
there's a better way*

and to

Pamela & Paul

Introduction

Much has been written about the merits and misgivings of strategic planning as a management tool. Every issue of *Business Week* has a strategy section, and articles on strategic planning appear frequently in *Fortune, Forbes,* the *Harvard Business Review,* and almost every other major business publication. Entire consulting practices have been founded and continue to flourish selling one product – strategic planning in every imaginable flavor: "How to," "When to," "What a strategic planner looks like," and most recently, "How to implement." Such prestigious firms as McKinsey, Arthur D. Little, Booz-Allen, the Boston Consulting Group, and most of the Big Eight accounting firms are called upon frequently, at tremendous fees, to help some likewise pretty big and prestigious enterprises to plan better.

What is it about this simple process of planning that is so difficult to understand and put into practice? In most cases it tends to be just an old-fashioned breakdown in communications, and a loss of objectivity by the management team. One of the things that I've noticed in large companies where I have worked and small companies where I have been a consultant is that senior managers tend to spend more time competing with each other than with their competitors. Once you're caught up in that familiar old political jousting match, objectivity disappears, and finger pointing and fire fighting become the order of the day. When you spend more time every day worrying and scheming about how you are going to make one of your corporate peers look bad than thinking about the marketplace; your competitors in that market; and being a good manager, then something is definitely wrong, and it permeates the entire organization, affects the company image, and eventually, the firm's ability to remain a viable competitor.

Corporate culture, another concept directly related to good planning, has also just recently received a lot of publicity in the form of articles, books, and seminars – when in reality, it too is as old and obvious as good commonsense planning. A good corporate culture and shared values can only come about when there is a basis for establishing that culture that also creates shared values. When everyone in management is working diligently on their own plans, and none of those plans are properly articulated or brought to the corporate round table for discussion, then the success or failure of the company rests with the most politically adroit — and not with the best managers, best plan, and what's best for all of the company's constituents.

Planning is probably the major activity that we all know we should do better. The purpose of this book is to explain: how strategic planning works; how to do it right; what to expect and what not to expect; how long it takes; who the players are and how they have to cooperate and interact; the role of the CEO; forms; and formats, using actual examples, pitfalls, and commentary from those who have tried to do it right.

The major disappointments with planning have come from those who were looking for another quick fix, or for someone to come in and put the plan together for them. These managers have expected too much, and frequently, the wrong things. Planning is hard work that takes time and requires input from those who have the most to lose and gain. Planning is getting people to do what they are supposed to be doing anyway — thinking, writing, and managing.

Planning does not eliminate risk; it minimizes it. It cannot predict the future with accuracy or prevent mistakes, but it can reduce the number and magnitude of surprises, and can provide contingency plans for the occurrence of both favorable and unfavorable situations. Managers should evaluate planning more by their ability to anticipate and effectively react to a changing environment than by how close they come to making their current financial targets at the expense of long-term survival.

One of the major problems that has to be overcome to get people started planning the right way is convincing them that they have to do three things they inherently dislike: taking time away from what they like to do, thinking, and writing those thoughts down. Nobody ever has any time to plan because they're fire fighting, even though they know that if they take the time now it will probably save time in the future. Planning is not deciding what to do in the future; it is deciding what to do now in order to have a future. That decision making process takes time. The thinking that goes into that decision making process takes time. You cannot think and work at the same time. One of the immediate benefits of planning is that it requires you to step back from day-to-day operations and gives you an opportunity to think more clearly. These thoughts also should be written down so they can be shared, critiqued, and reviewed again at a later date. Unwritten planning thoughts are like daydreams — they're only good for a day, or for as long as that mental imprint lasts.

You start the planning process by taking the time to find out where you are with your business and what is going on around you. There is no way that you can evaluate trends and study market conditions when you are constantly fire fighting. You lose objectivity as a result of being too close to the day-to-day business. This first step is generally referred to as "determining your strengths and weaknesses." The next step is thinking about what kind of business you would like to have at some time in the future. After that evaluation of where you are now and where you want to be over time, you can develop plans on how and when you are going to get there. Basically, planning is deciding why you are going to do something before you do it, rather than the easier way of doing something and then trying to figure out why you did it.

While there is no rigidly standard recipe for planning, there are some fundamental questions that are applicable to almost all planning exercises: "Where are we now?" "Where do we want to go?" "How are we going to get there?" "When will we arrive?" "Who will be responsible for what?" "How much will each step cost? ' and "What will we accept as a reasonable return for each investment along the way?" Strategic planning is taking these questions to the management team in a rigorous exercise that forces them to answer these questions and to hold themselves accountable for making it happen.

Good strategic planning draws the management team together and doles out "what-if" assignments, the answers to which, and the accompanying analysis, create action plans that are well thought-out and have a reasonable chance of success. This work of assessing strengths, weaknesses, and the capacity to change, and then looking out into the future and establishing what kind of a business the team wants, isn't easy. Then, working back in time, developing strategies to get from where you are to where you want to be, is really challenging. That is probably why many CEOs reject the practicality of conscious strategy making and prefer to preside over undeclared or intuitive strategies that have never been articulated or analyzed.

If a management team has no way of creating its future, then they adapt to whatever happens on a day-to-day basis. Improvisation becomes their limited strategy, and the planning horizon continues to be next week, next month, and next year. One of the best performance evaluation systems for appraising the quality of management is measuring their ability, over time, to execute a demanding strategy that is constantly being tested in the marketplace. With a plan you manage the plan; without one you manage from day to day.

So planning, in its simplest state, is setting a course for your company that is well thought-out by the management team; measuring progress against that plan; and updating the plan based upon your ability to achieve it. Budgeting is an integral part of the planning process, but a budget is really not a plan. It is the month-by-month quantifiable goals that have to be accomplished to have a plan. It is the control vehicle by which management measures progress toward their longer-term strategic goals.

Well-managed Fortune 500 companies practice strategic planning, and continue to demonstrate its effectiveness in their publicity releases. For these management groups, planning is an integral part of managing, and it has effectively systematized the management process. However, this technique is not solely the preserve of the big boys, and this book explains how anyone can utilize these concepts of tactics and strategy.

There should be general agreement that planning and budgeting go hand in hand, and that the annual business plan is no longer an effective way to manage in the 80s. Strategic planning reverses the historical perspective of looking from last year to this year to next year, by looking out beyond next year and the year after and establishing future goals, and then working back in time and developing strategies to get from where you are to where you want to be. Then the annual plan becomes the first step towards those future objectives, and the exercise of strategies guides the business towards those goals.

The essence of good planning is asking "Why?" and "Then what?" until what has to be done to get from where you are to where you want to be becomes crystal clear. During recent years, planning has changed in nature, scope, and purpose. Managers are beginning to appreciate the significance of the military saying: "Plans are sometimes useless, but the planning process is indispensable." They used to think the sole purpose of planning was to produce a plan. Now they are starting to realize that "a plan" is a valuable by-product (if it is flexible enough to respond to rapidly changing conditions); but the primary purpose of planning is to provide a better way of reaching and revising agreement. This requires a dynamic planning process.

The success of any planning effort depends upon active support by top management combined with a process for planning that makes it possible for key personnel to participate effectively. This cannot be accomplished overnight. It should not be attempted on a crash basis or without understanding the time, effort, and cost required to achieve acceptable results. Some of the best results have come from the use of outside professionals during the initial design and implementation period. In this way, time and money can be saved, mistakes and frustrations avoided, and improved operational results achieved sooner.

While there is no standard guide for planning that comes in a video cassette that can be used by all organizations, there are certain planning concepts and techniques that do have universal acceptance. This book attempts to capture a proven process that has been thoroughly tested by the author and by many other practitioners, and does work. As planning is, in most cases, an inherently political process, the techniques discussed throughout this book create progress in terms of team and time.

In the final analysis, while the process may be similar for most organizations, the final plan tends to be rather customized to the climate and culture of each organization.

Contents

1
Strategic Planning Explained

Strategic planning, or, strategy making, is a technique that chief executives of any size business can use to identify and deal with concerns that they have about the future of their business. These concerns are usually difficult to identify, and are clearly disturbing, and have been for some time. This feeling is a result of one of the following situations:

1. The business is deteriorating.
2. The business is growing out of control.
3. Crisis management is standard operating procedure.

Unfortunately, widespread confusion exists over just how to define strategic planning. To some, it's a glorified repackaging of old-fashioned business planning, and to others, it's just a modification of long-range planning. While it includes elements of both, strategic planning is really a management system that allows managers to focus more clearly on the most important aspects of their business.

Strategic planning bridges the gap between the annual business plan and the traditional long-range plan. From an overall perspective, the strategic planning process integrates elements of three management planning concepts: the annual business plan, diversification planning, and long-range planning. A strategic plan establishes the parameters for an organization's future growth, and gives management the ability to quantify and measure progress. Specifically, a strategic plan considers the outlook for each component of a business — product by product and market by market — and establishes realistic goals based on detailed analysis of the markets, competition, technology, the economy, and other significant factors.

Long-range planning, on the other hand, usually consists of straight line extrapolations of existing data to meet acceptable growth rates

1

and financial ratios. The typical result is the well-known "hockey stick effect" in which the growth rate for the next five years equals at least twice that of the last five years. A strategic plan eliminates much of this artificial growth projection by requiring an objective assessment of the business. Management must both ask and answer tough questions about all aspects of the business: "What..." "How ..." "Why..." etc.

Diversification planning, for many companies, is an activity separate from the annual business plan (and from the long-range plan, if the organization has one). Diversification planning, in most cases, turns out to be a relatively unorganized search for new products, new technology, new processes, and new businesses. Many diversification efforts result in diluting the base business by getting companies involved in products, markets, or businesses unrelated to their historical management strengths and business experiences. Diversification plans should be a natural by-product of the strategic planning process, and a strategy, or strategies, of the overall plan — not a separate activity.

The annual business plan, or annual budget, is not really an effective planning instrument. It focuses exclusively on next year's results, and sets forth performance measures, in terms of sales, profits, expense ratios, and inventory levels, that define acceptable levels needed to "meet plan," but just for one year. Information for annual plans usually only comes from sales forecasts of customer requirements and analyses of short-term economic conditions.

In contrast, a strategic plan contains multiyear market forecasts that identify key product areas for development, as well as technological, competitive, and regulatory trends influencing market growth for the next year, and the years beyond. In addition, a strategic plan is more flexible than an annual plan, specifying critical milestones and decision points over the strategic plan period.

EARLY STRATEGIC PLANNING

The first form of strategic planning was a combination of the annual budget and the long-range plan. The result was a monstrous number-crunching exercise that seemed to take forever. It did, however, force planners to ask more questions about the "sense" of the exercise. Over the last several years, this nonintegrated combination has been refined into a sophisticated planning process that is being used successfully in small and medium-sized companies, as well as in the Fortune 500. Good business managers in any sized company know that just straightlining last year's experience won't work anymore. Sure, there will be inflationary growth, but where is the real growth coming from? Strategic planning clarifies these issues and can provide the answer.

To be successful, a strategic planning exercise needs the support and involvement of management — everyone from the CEO to the junior managers. Without their commitment, the process becomes an exercise in futility that can do more harm than good. The potential for positive results is considerable when everyone works together for the betterment of themselves and the organization. In recent surveys polling CEOs on the rewards derived from formal planning, almost all reported that planning helps them establish a more definitive view of the future, as it enables them to better balance the short-term with the long-term. Said one chief executive, "It helps ensure that all guns are pointed at the same target."

The strategic planning process benefits a business in several ways.

- It assembles an effective management team.
- It marshalls an organization's resources toward very specific goals.
- It creates an excellent performance measurement and appraisal system for management.
- It generates a thorough analysis of business strengths and weaknesses.
- It forces on managers a needed discipline that makes them better managers.

In many businesses, one of the best benefits to come from the strategic planning process is not the plan itself, but the process. Getting top management to think and act like a team is a very special success. Interviews with managers at all levels in strategically managed companies reveal four common themes.

1. The value of teamwork is greatly enhanced and creates task-oriented organizational flexibility.
2. Entrepreneurial drive is reborn in a common commitment to making things happen.
3. Open communications creates a healthier climate than the preservation of confidentiality.
4. A good feeling that the company can really create its own future, rather than be driven by a variety of external forces, emerges.

Combining these positive attitudes with a good strategic plan enables a business to capitalize on strengths and minimize weaknesses.

THE STRATEGY IN PLANNING

What's the "strategy" behind this kind of planning? The management team gets together to focus on current strengths and weaknesses in terms of:

- Products
- Markets
- Customers
- Finances
- Technology
- Management

This assessment is combined with reasonable estimates of the shape of the business at some time in the near future — typically, up to five years. "Strategies" are the action plans to get the business from where it is to where management would like it to be at the end of the strategic planning period. These strategies need to be "priced-out" they must be:

Economically Viable. A thorough analysis of conservative projections results in projected returns that satisfy the financial criteria for return on assets and reinvestment plans.

Achievable. Past experience, the resources allocated, and management strengths related to specific strategies are taken into consideration. The goals are achievable under normal operating conditions.

Manageable. After time-phasing and properly prioritizing strategies, the company can manage the base business and prudently implement the strategic plan.

A typical strategy contains the following information.

1. what it is (an explanation of the strategy).
2. why it is (the rationale for the strategy).
3. who is responsible for managing the strategy.
4. how much it will cost.
5. how long it will take (with quarterly milestones).
6. what return is expected (ROI).

As an example, the time-phasing of a strategy would be:

STRATEGY: PACKAGING MODERNIZATION FOR WIDGETS

What: 1. The widget product line is to be repackaged in a modern style to create a new image. The new package design will be supported by advertising and promotional materials.

Why: 2. Over the last two years it has become more and more apparent that the decline in sales of our widget product line can be attributed to consumers perceiving widgets becoming "the product we used to use" in that funny looking old cardboard box. This has been verified by a variety of market research studies and by the loss of shelf space to competitors who have switched to the less expensive, easier to use, and more attractive variety of light plastic containers. In order to regain market share and position widgets for the future, we have to implement this strategy.

Who: 3. Tom Smith, product manager widgets, has the total responsibility for implementation of this strategy.

How
Much: 4. The cost of the strategy has been projected to be:

$ 75,000	Package design and production of prototypes
15,000	Modification of production line
30,000	Write-off of obsolete product and packaging
100,000	Advertising — Newspapers and key magazines
40,000	Promotional materials and samples
15,000	Contingency
$275,000	TOTAL

How
Long: 5. Twelve months broken down into:

> *First Quarter* — Select agency;
> *Second Quarter* — Select design, review and approve prototypes;
> *Third Quarter* — Schedule production of new design. Approve advertising and promotional program. Final management approval; and
> *Fourth Quarter* — Implement strategy and evaluate initial results.

Expected
Return: 6. The expected return is that sales will reach $675,000 at the end of the first full year after the strategy has been implemented, which will give widgets 18 percent of the market.

Earnings over the first three years after strategy implementation are projected to total $41,250, for a 15 percent return on the investment in this strategy.

This clearly spells out the objective and the plan for reaching the objective.

Each strategy must be time-phased once it has met the aforementioned criteria. The only way that strategic plans will be successful is if careful and sensible quarterly milestones are established for every strategy. If a strategy is to modernize the image of a product line with new packaging and a supporting advertising and promotional campaign, an example of the timing of strategic milestones for such a strategy would be:

QUARTER	MILESTONE	MANAGER	EXPECTED COMPLETION DATE
First	Research and schedule presentations from creative packaging agencies	T. Smith	End of February
	Evaluate and select agency		End of March
Second	Review agency recommendations with management	T. Smith	Middle of May
	Commit to new package design and budget for design phase		End of May
	Review and approve prototypes		End of June
Third	Begin development of advertising and promotional campaign		Middle of July
	Schedule production of new packaging to coincide with:		
	1. Depletion of existing stock 2. Implementation of advertising and promotion campaign		End of July
	Present new packaging design and outline of promotional campaign to sales managers		End of August
	Approve sequence of advertising schedule and promotional campaign		Middle of September
	Final management approval of entire program		End of September
Fourth	Launch campaign		Middle of October
	Evaluate initial impact and potential to achieve the overall goals of the strategy		Middle of December

THE MISSION STATEMENT

With the business objectives established and strategies determined, management is on its way to giving the organization a well-thought-out and agreed-to direction that can be quantified and measured. It's now possible to create a mission statement for the organization. A mission statement is a written explanation of the purposes of the business. It presents its goals in terms of:

- Products
- Markets
- Competitive posture
- Management philosophy
- Ethics
- Social responsibility

This statement must be specific and clear, and can be a substantial accomplishment in itself. It can't be written until the entire exercise is complete, since it sums up the various elements that have gone into the planning process. Reaching the point of a completed mission statement is a major effort for the uninitiated, and can take six to nine months to accomplish, if the strategic planning process is begun from zero.

A question often asked is, "How long is the strategic planning period?" The answer to that question rests with management. How long can the CEO look out into the future, within reason? Typically, strategic plans are about five years' worth of an attempt to plan for the future. In reality, it takes about that long to effect any real change in a business. In addition, it takes about three years to implement totally an effective strategic planning *process* in almost any business. Managing a strategic plan is at least as important as developing one. Unlike long-range plans, which often are put on the shelf and dusted off every few years, strategic plans are action-oriented, flexible working tools.

2
How a Small Business Can Start the Strategic Planning Process

For small to medium-sized business managers, there seems to be some mystique surrounding the concept of strategic planning. They seem to think that strategic planning is a big-business concept. This probably happens because sole proprietors and entrepreneurs, for the most part, are so busy with growing and minding their business that they haven't taken the time to study modern management techniques. Consequently, words like *strategic* and *planning* are virtually foreign to them, because they don't plan, and they have no real strategies other than those locked away in the deep recesses of their minds.

There are common threads that run through all unplanned businesses.

1. They have a very hard time developing good new business opportunities internally.
2. They waste valuable resources by constantly subsidizing "brainstorm" ideas that are not thoroughly analyzed before they are implemented.
3. They underinvest time and resources in their most profitable products.
4. They fail to fund adequately their existing growth opportunities.

Almost all businesses can benefit from strategic planning: all sizes of manufacturing firms, and service firms as well. How does a company get started? It usually starts with the CEO, general manager, or board of directors getting bitten by the planning bug. This happens in a variety of ways: through seminars; reading about success stories; or in discussions with other businessmen at the club or at a trade association meeting. However it happens, it has to be brought to fruition by some external force for the most successful planning experience to occur. There are four ways to get started: (1) contract with a professional strategic planning organization or management consulting association; (2) hire a strategic planner as an employee; (3) hire a professional strategic planning consultant to facilitate the process; or (4) select an easy-to-use primer and follow the step-by-step process, while learning how to overcome obstacles and avoid pitfalls. Each of these techniques to begin planning has advantages and disadvantages of which the CEO should be aware. These are as follows.

USE A STRATEGIC PLANNING ORGANIZATION

ADVANTAGES:

1. Thorough and detailed approach
2. Professional critique of the business
3. Management education for the staff

DISADVANTAGES:

1. Professionals tend to intimidate the staff
2. Too much – too fast
3. Professionally developed plan for implementation – but how?

HIRE A STRATEGIC PLANNER

ADVANTAGES:

1. Member of the team wants it to work
2. Always around to explain and assist
3. Manages implementation

DISADVANTAGES:

1. May become intimidated like the other employees
2. May become frustrated by the lack of professionalism, dedication, or the return to a "business as usual" attitude
3. May intimidate, aggravate, or turn off other members of the team – new kid on the block

USE A STRATEGIC PLANNING CONSULTANT

ADVANTAGES:

1. Usually more flexible in their timing for the exercise
2. Willing to customize the process to the company's culture
3. Works well one-on-one with other members of the management team

DISADVANTAGES:

1. A lone consultant is usually working on other projects simultaneously — can result in a time conflict
2. How to find the "right" one — hard to find
3. Tends to become "their plan" for "your business" — who implements?

SELECT A PRIMER AS A GUIDE

ADVANTAGES:

1. Can study the process several times before beginning
2. Become aware of potential obstacles and know of pitfalls before beginning
3. Can practice and create the process on paper as a basis for comparison before involving the staff

DISADVANTAGES:

1. CEO not only has to be involved and committed, but also must be the instrument — difficult dual role
2. There is no substitute for experience
3. Hard to eliminate natural bias when trying to change the way you and your staff thinks

Regardless of how it's implemented, the strategic planning process follows the general pattern that follows.

HAVE AN ORIENTATION SESSION FOR THE STAFF

In any case, the strategic planning process starts with an orientation for the staff on the concepts of strategic planning. It is critical to the success of any strategic planning activity to have the CEO's staff (direct reports) participate together in the orientation session, to share in the common experience and become familiar with strategic planning terms. At the beginning, the terminology of planning will be different, and everybody will have to start speaking a new language. Eventually, the management team will even start to *think* differently, and strategically.

The orientation usually takes a full day, but can be done in a half-day session. It is imperative to have the orientation and as many other sessions as possible "off-site," preferably in a nearby motel with conference facilities.

It is critical to the success of any planning endeavor to allow sufficient amounts of uninterrupted time for planning. The very essence of planning is creative thinking, discussion amongst the management team, consensus building, and good solid analysis. To accomplish this kind of a meeting of minds takes uninterrupted time. There cannot be ringing phones and messages delivered by conscientious secretaries on little pieces of paper. It's impossible to do any kind of serious planning and run the business at the same time. All major planning sessions should take place away from the office.

ANALYZE STRENGTHS AND WEAKNESSES

At the end of the orientation, the management team is assigned to fill out, objectively and independently, internal and external strategic audit worksheets. Exhibit 2.1 is the internal strengths and weaknesses worksheet; it has been completed with actual company data, as an example. This form is the most important initial step in the process, and to produce the best results, should be completed objectively and without consulting other members of the management team. If done properly, it will establish the common strengths and weaknesses of the business.

Exhibit 2.2 is the external strategic audit worksheet, which also contains actual responses from one management team, and requires input on: technology developments, by-product potential, sales potential, and key performance indicators. This information will reflect the level of future thinking about current trends on the part of the management team.

Exhibit 2.1 Internal Strategic Audit Worksheet

PREPARED BY: Charles Smith   **TITLE** ___V.P. Marketing___   **DATE** _____

DIVISION, BUSINESS UNIT, SUBSIDIARY: _____XYZ Company_____

Strengths:	1.	Experienced, cooperative management team.
	2.	High-quality product line.
	3.	Good financial control system.
	4.	Strong position in international market.
	5.	Good manufacturing capabilities and flexibility.
	6.	Excellent service and parts distribution system.
Weaknesses:	1.	Decline in brand awareness and market research efforts.
	2.	Weak and geographically limited dealer network.
	3.	Inability to forecast accurately.
	4.	React to competitive moves rather than initiate.
	5.	High cost producer.
	6.	Slow-moving inventory hurts cash flow.

NOTE: Be specific, clear and concise, but most of all, be critical and objective.
It is in your best interest to make a better company and business plan.
You do not have to have six of each, so don't be creative. However, if
there are some other things, add them here:

___No plan_____

___Willingness of employees to just accept the status quo._____

_____

Exhibit 2.2   External Strategic Audit Worksheet

Technology
Projection:

What do you see happening in your area of the business that represents a
technological threat?

Improved grass collection techniques.

Chemical growth retardants.

Diesel manufacturers offering more hydrostatic/syncromesh transmissions.

Changes in power sources: battery vs. electric vs. gas.

Impact of CAD-CAM systems on product development.

By-product
Projection:

What other by-products do you think our company could make and market,
given what you know about the market and our company's manufacturing
capacity?

Any all-purpose vehicle that uses motors and transmissions.

Become and OEM for government.

Sales
Expansion:

Do you see any way to expand the geographic area that the salesmen cover
to increase volume profitably?

Open new dealers in weak or no presence territories.

Develop a national account – private label program.

Key
Performance
Indicators:

What are the most important indicators to you as to how business is going
for a given month or quarter?

Bookings and backlog.

Inventory turnover.

Days of receivables outstanding.

New accounts.

Exhibit 2.3 External Strategic Audit Worksheet

CUSTOMERS YOU WOULD LIKE TO HAVE	COMPETITOR WHO HAS THEM	POSSIBLE STRATEGY TO GET SOME OF THEIR BUSINESS
John Deere –	Lawn Boy	Price/Features Analysis
Mowers		
Ford Ag	Gilson	Presentation of quality of our products to those
Dealers		dealers.
National	Various	Special targeted programs – price sensitive.
(Sears, etc.)		
Competitors –	Lawn Boy	Concentrate on weakest aspects of their products
Dealers	Ariens	and dealer network.
	Wheel Horse	

These questionnaires are the first step in beginning the strategic planning process and getting management to think strategically. They are also the first step in the sorting out of managerial excellence amongst the management team, because the quality of the responses is usually indicative of each manager's competence and knowledge of the total business.

Objectivity is the key to success in a good evaluation of strengths and weaknesses. When evaluations are done well, the same several strengths and weaknesses will appear, and in that case, they will be representative of the real situation in the business, because everybody who is serious about their career and the business they are involved in will be sincerely interested in contributing to any effort that will make the business better. If you don't develop a realistic picture of the business, you can't develop a plan to take advantage of the company's strengths or to overcome its weaknesses. Self-appraisal for the management team is not easy. Many senior managers are not prepared to accept the fact that they have been managing weaknesses.

In addition, it's good to get some input on competitors, which is usually referred to as competitive analysis. Exhibit 2.3 outlines three critical factors that have to be addressed to get the management team to think strategically. First, list the *customers you would like to have;* most companies are content with the customers they have and don't have any strategies on how to get customers from their competitors. The only way to get started here is to draw up a list of the customers you would like to have and along with that the *competitor who* currently *has them.* Then you can complete this form by developing *possible strategies to get some of their business.* If you haven't thought along these lines before, it can be a very worthwhile exercise.

Another part of doing good competitive analysis is completing Exhibit 2.4, which requires the listing of all of your *competitors, their products,* and *prices* they charge for those products; and then going on to try to evaluate their level of *service* and their *sales* staff. In the process of evaluating your competitors in this way, you may just strike upon some other interesting strategies for yourself. Competitive analysis seems to be one of those aspects of business that managers take for granted. They seem content to assume that their competitors have been around for about the same length of time that *they* have, and that they've been doing about the same things. In every industry, most companies do do about the same things year in and year out, but there are also companies in those same industries which are busy working diligently to achieve the competitive advantage through stragety making.

Another often misunderstood concept of competitive analysis is developing the *profile of your perfect customer.* An example of this concept would be:

PROFILING THE PERFECT CUSTOMER

Product by Product

Product	*Customer Profile Questions*
Widgets	1. Why do they buy widgets?
	2. How many widgets do they use in their business/ home?
	3. How many of them are there?
	4. Where are they located?
	5. What publications are they most likely to get?
	6. Why would they use our widgets over our competitor's?
	7. Can we determine what incentive is the key to their purchasing decisions?
	8. Can we provide that incentive?

Everybody thinks that whoever buys the most is your "best" customer, or whoever buys the "most profitable" mix of products is your best customer. These assumptions can often be misconceptions. It's better to develop a profile of who your perfect customer should be, and then go out and try to find that kind of customer to sell your products to. These are the beginnings of market segmentation study and marketing planning, natural by-products of strategic planning and portfolio analysis.

Since thought and research are necessary to assemble the needed information accurately and completely, allow several days or weeks between the orientation meeting and distribution of the forms, and the next meeting. Be sure the participants understand that they're to respond objectively and independently — the consensus will come later.

AGREE ON STRATEGIES

The next meeting is for reviewing the strengths and weaknesses. The routine at this meeting is that each member of the management team

Exhibit 2.4 External Strategic Audit Worksheet

COMPETITORS	PRODUCTS	PRICE	SERVICE	SALESMEN
JOHN DEERE	Agriculture/Industrial/ Consumer. Full line of products (gas/diesel)	Medium to High, but offer consumer/retail financing	Excellent – *all* dealers well-trained	Direct to dealer/Block-type system
SEARS	Consumer Products (no diesel) – but full line of gas products	Low to Medium consumer retail/financing	Poor to Medium – Use outside sources Small engine people	Vary in product knowledge
KUBOTA	Diesel products, 15 HP up to 72 HP; and track vehicles	Low to High – very competitive. Starting consumer financing	Good quality dealer converts from Ford/ IH, etc.	Direct to retailer Well-trained in diesel products
LAWN BOY	Lawn mowers; edgers; dropped out of riders/ snow	Low to High (including Ryan) Steel and cast decks – own two cycle engine	Excellent in field service as well as factory back-up	Most markets: Distribute to dealer. Some: direct to dealer
TORO	Lawn mowers; snow riders; trimmers; irriga-tion equipment; turf equipment	Medium to High	Good to Excellent	Distribute to dealers Most distributors sell Toro product only
SNAPPER	Lawn mowers; riders; snow tractors	Medium to High	Good to Excellent	Distribute to dealers In south sell Snapper only

Exhibit 2.4   External Strategic Audit Worksheet (cont.)

COMPETITORS	PRODUCTS	PRICE	SERVICE	SALESMEN
HONDA	Mowers; snow throwers; generators; engines. Introducing steel deck mowers, lawn tractors	High To meet middle price range	Good to Excellent	Selling direct to dealer Selective marketing
SIMPLICITY	Full line gasoline power product manufacturing. Imports two diesel products. All gas products made by Simplicity	Medium to High	Good to Excellent	Sell through distributor and direct
WHEEL HORSE	Gasoline ride-on products	Was Medium to High – Now changing to Low to Medium	Recent dealer complaints; was Good to Excellent	Direct to dealer with infrequent on-site
GILSON	Full line gasoline power product manufacturing – both branded and private label	Low to Medium	Good	Diversified depending on business area
ARIENS	Full line gasoline power product manufacturers. Just acquired Ford-Bolens-Toro	Medium to High	Good to Excellent	Sell through distributor
PRIVATE LABEL	Cover *all* gasoline product lines	Low to Medium – priced to market	Fair to Good – Small engine repair shops	Sell directly to national and regional chains

presents his/her perception of the company's strengths and weaknesses. The consultant, facilitator, or management organization representative usually writes these down on a flip chart as they are presented.

In the process of making the presentations on strengths and weaknesses, it usually becomes quite obvious to the CEO that there are some members of the management team that have a very different perception of strengths and weaknesses than he does. This, in itself, becomes valuable input to building or rebuilding the team concept. More importantly, it sets the stage for reaching consensus on what the management team as a group really feels are the strengths and weaknesses of their common endeavor. For some members of senior management, this can be an extremely enlightening experience.

Once consensus has been reached, the next planning assignment is given out. Each member of the management team is requested to take the respective strengths and/or weaknesses related to his/her area of responsibility, or to an all-inclusive team responsibility, and develop action plans (strategies) to make the strengths "more and better" and to improve the weaknesses. Exhibit 2.5 is an illustration of a format for this phase of the initial planning exercise, that has been completed with some actual case history data. This part of the planning exercise is more time-consuming than the initial exercise because it requires serious thinking, given the parameters of the company's resources. To some extent, it should also function as a "should do," or "wish list" to make the business better. It should be the beginning of focusing management direction towards the future. Up to this point they have been collecting information about how their business is *now.* In thinking about current strengths and weaknesses and developing action programs to deal with them, you are forming a natural basis for projecting where the company is going. As the exercise continues, the management team will formulate a conceptual overview of where they want the business to be at some time in the future.

These proposed action programs are reviewed at the next meeting of the strategic planning team, which takes place after another mutually agreeable time interval. This meeting almost always produces a list of programs that is extensive and ranges from "brainstorming" ideas

Exhibit 2.5 Internal Strategic Audit Worksheet

Strengths and Weaknesses — Programs for Improvement

STRENGTHS	WEAKNESSES
1. Brand position — *Program A.* Advertising exposure consistent with quality; B. Communicate positiveness of company and its products	1. Low market share — *Program A.* Acquire complimentary products; B. Increase outlets in primary distribution channel; C. Target accounts from other distribution channels
2. Worldwide presence — *Program A.* Channel more product through organization	2. Underutilization of capacity — *Program A.* Acquire complimentary (to process) products; B. Develop contract manufacturing business
3. Captive sales force — *Program A.* Enhance and develop effectiveness; B. Increase recognition; C. Complimentary products	3. Cost position is too high — *Program A.* Effective cost improvement program; B. Increased absorption; C. Volume, design, process trade-offs
4. Independent status — *Program A.* Responsiveness; B. Flexibility	4. Limited financial resources — *Program A.* Secure additional equity; B. Increase utilization of assets
5. — *Program*	5. Product development process – penalties — *Program A.* System of checks and balances to control; B. Better planning
6. — *Program*	6. Company image — *Program A.* Positive communication of company philosophy; B. Product development
	7. Willingness to accept status quo — *Program A.* Task/challenging objectives

to almost impossible-to-achieve futuristic projects. The planning consultant, or advisor, puts all of these programs on a flip chart. Then each program is evaluated by the entire team, and a priority list is prepared based upon the following criteria:

1. Importance to sustaining and profitably enlarging the existing business.
2. Significance to future growth:
    a. Technology.
    b. Competitive posture.
    c. By-products of existing business.
    d. Acquisition/Divestiture.
3. Research investment in new products, processes, and ventures.
4. Management's ability to deal with the project, given existing resources, talent, and priority assigned to other projects.
5. Level of success in achieving similar objectives in the past.

During the evaluation, the facilitator points out that the objective of the exercise is to come up with viable and achievable strategies that will result in establishing a firm base of manageable, profitable business opportunities. With this in mind, this usually extensive list of ideas is reduced to seven or eight key proposals that make sense and can be accomplished.

It's important to make sure that your plan is as realistic as possible, complete, and internally consistent. The success of the plan is critical to your company's future. The most in-depth review possible will contribute to the plan's effectiveness as a whole. Assessing the achievability of your strategic goals is the major challenge of planning.

One of the dangers any management group faces in starting the planning process is setting very ambitious initial goals, falling short, and becoming disenchanted with the entire planning process. For this reason, especially with the first planning exercise, it has to be kept very simple, practical, and within reasonable objectives.

PRICE-OUT THE STRATEGIES

After the most important proposals are agreed upon, the next assignment is distributed: that is, taking these proposals, each by the responsible manager, to "price-out" and "time-phase" them. Depending upon order of magnitude, this phase of the planning exercise can take from several weeks to a month. This is usually a functional exercise that requires a fair amount of evaluation, research, and conceptual thinking.

This may involve thinking through new marketing strategies, expanding into different parts of the country (or the world), creating by-products, developing innovative new applications, upgrading manufacturing processes (for example, transition to robots), developing a new image, or launching extensive training programs to upgrade staff. All of these issues require thinking and planning time, and trying to answer difficult questions like "Can we really do it?" However, this is invaluable time spent exploring potential projects that can result in survival, or in substantial changes in direction. It may be the first time that this kind of creative thinking has happened.

These potential projects may also result in capital expenditures, addition of staff, or revamping operations and administrative procedures — all of which have to be thoroughly thought out.

SELECT THE MOST PROMISING POTENTIAL STRATEGIES

When all the work is done, the team gets back together and reviews the results. During the evaluation stage, some projects may be determined to be too expensive, or impossible to achieve; others may be expanded; and some new, or modified programs may emerge. This round of review usually is extensive, and involves the presentation of alternatives. It is the most time-consuming and important phase of the planning exercise.

Out of this evaluation process by the management team will come those strategies that will make up the nucleus of the initial strategic plan. They will be priced-out in terms of expenditures and expected returns, as well as time-phased by quarter. It is also important to get a commitment from each manager who will be responsible for implementing these strategies, because those commitments should be folded into their respective compensation plans.

Part of the value associated with strategic planning is the ability to marry compensation planning for management with the achievement of strategic milestones. It is the essence of an effective performance appraisal system for management.

MISSION STATEMENT

Up to this point, the planning exercise has focused on identifying where the business is now (strengths and weaknesses) and what has to be done to get the company from where it is to where it wants to be, or to a more solid base of operations, so that there is a vehicle in place to get to where management would like to be. This rigorous process of taking the time to think, evaluate, analyze, and concur on a course of action as a *team* is what strategic planning is all about. It is the process of evaluating products, markets, competition, and managerial competence. It is creating alternative business opportunities, new products, by-products, new markets, and developing the scenario and steps necessary to make those things happen. Strategic planning requires intuitive and conceptual thinking. It changes the way management thinks, allocates, and reallocates resources as time progresses.

And, it requires writing. That writing takes two different but related forms: a mission statement and an initial operating plan. The mission statement is designed to capture the results of the planning exercise in an explanation of the company's purpose in being. It is a clear statement as to what management believes the company is in existence to accomplish. The mission statement should be an all-encompassing discussion of:

1. The current and planned configuration of business objectives relating to products, markets, and competitive posture.
2. Management's philosophy as to their commitment to employees, stockholders, and the community. Their policies on ethics, social responsibility, and the environment.
3. The financial growth goals and objectives of the organization.

The mission statement is an important product of the strategic planning process. It is the embodiment of management's purpose in being together as a team, the course they have set for the business, and the managerial philosophy that sets the theme for the present, and for the future of the organization.

A typical mission statement written by the management team of a $10 million manufacturing company (XYZ Industries, Inc., for this purpose) which has completed its first strategic planning exercise, is as follows:

XYZ INDUSTRIES, INC.

MISSION STATEMENT

XYZ Industries is an organization of dedicated individuals devoted to developing and delivering the highest quality products and services to the graphic arts industry, as well as exploring peripheral industrial applications that fit their innovative services and technological know-how. This concentrated research of applications for XYZ's technological strengths and new emerging products is designed to open new markets and create opportunities for by-products of the existing manufacturing processes.

XYZ is ideally positioned to react to changing technology and maintain a leadership position in gravure engraving and lithographic color separation services for the graphic arts industry by maintaining an aggressive research and development effort on new processes related to the graphic arts industry, and by imaginative constant review of these processes for other industrial and commercial use.

Part of the overall mission of XYZ management is to continue to improve the climate for employees, reward initiative, and provide incentives to increase job satisfaction, productivity, and to encourage individual development. This emphasis on management development is designed to maintain a highly motivated and professional management team and staff.

Within this framework of competitive marketing and research planning, XYZ's financial mission is to continue to increase net worth with sales and earnings growth equal to or greater than 15 percent annually over the foreseeable planning horizon, with cash flow sufficient to support growth requirements.

Future acquisitions will only be considered if they offer a unique, competitive opportunity at an extremely attractive price, or if they will result in upgrading XYZ's resources and technology significantly.

XYZ Industries is committed to being a good neighbor in the communities in which it operates, and maintains the highest standards of ethics and social responsibility in the conduct of its business.

The mission statement is usually written by the chief executive, using all of the results of the strategic planning exercise. Since the chief executive has the overall responsibility for management and guidance of the company, the mission tends to be his/her mission to accomplish.

Once the mission statement is complete, the business or operating plan can be developed. The mission statement sets the tone for the operating plan. Operating plans derived from initial strategic plans take a variety of written forms, based on how they are intended to be used by management. The most common form is a narrative outline of where management wants the business to be, and the steps they have taken to start managing the business in that direction. These steps encompass beginning the planning process, outlining the strengths and weaknesses, and arraying the strategies in a time-phased fashion.

A typical example would be the following excerpts from the XYZ Industries, Inc. Operating (Business) Plan.

Overview

In 198X, we completed the initial strategy planning exercise for XYZ Industries. This is the first time such an exercise has been attempted and we feel it will assist us greatly in achieving our future growth objectives.

Our plan for 198X calls for us to implement these strategies which will result in a concentrated set of marketing, production and product development plans. We expect to be able to better evaluate our product lines, our investment policies, and our people. We expect to improve greatly our management information systems which will, in turn, assist our managers in producing, delivering, and creating new and better products.

Our sales for 198X are projected at $XX,XXX, an increase of 9.7 percent over estimated 198X sales. Profits for 198X are projected at $XXX,XXX – compared to estimated 198X profits of $XXX,XXX after the $XXX,XXX "write-off" – an increase of 71.4 percent.

In 198X, we will be looking much more at sales via the "product line" approach. As you will see later in this plan, we not only have product lines listed by sales but have also developed individual P and L's by product line. Advantages of this type of reporting are obvious, but, to name a few, it will enable us to estimate return on investment by product line; evaluate our investments in equipment and people; and it will assist us in decisions related to marketing and pricing.

In our budgeting, we have attempted, for cash flow purposes, to be quite conservative. For the first time we are differentiating between corporate *budget* and corporate *sales quota.* The budget is what we minimally expect to accomplish. The "sales quota" is what we would like each of our sales people to produce. Salesman compensation has been improved in order to reflect this philosophy, i.e. higher pay for sales *quota* achievement. Although 'sales quotas" are not included in this report, they will run generally 15 percent above budgeted figures.

As for overall general economic forecasting for 198X, we are assuming that the recession will continue, at least in the housing area, throughout the first half of the year, and we have reduced the forecast in those areas accordingly. At the same time, we have and will continue to emphasize the selling and marketing functions of the company.

In our forecast from 198X through 198X, we have included numerous factors which influence the overall sales and profit results. These factors include:

1. Inflation.
2. Improved productive efficiency due to installation of new "state-of-the-art" equipment which is reflected primarily in production and direct labor rate.
3. Costs and charges related to updating of management.
4. Increased sales related to better sales and marketing management and increased number of sales personnel.

We have not included potential increase in sales and profits due to new product development and licensing agreements, although we feel that these may be very real factors in our future growth.

Marketing Summary

In the strategic plan there is a Marketing Summary and Objective for each of our product lines.

For XYZ as a whole, the general marketing strategy for increased sales will include the following:

1. Development of a professional, service-oriented sales staff — properly trained and properly motivated to achieve the highest quality and volume of sales.
2. Awareness and utilization of the latest techniques and technology to produce top quality products at the lowest possible cost.
3. Development of improved and new products and the successful marketing of same within our market range.
4. Expansion, as justified by market research, into new marketing areas, both geographically and by industry.
5. Utilization of the total XYZ facilities in the promotion and sales of its products.
6. Sales and profit by product lines, as listed in our product line profit and loss statement, will be used to evaluate each product line in terms of its value to the overall corporation — our first attempt at portfolio analysis.

Operating Plan 198X–8X

A.   Introduction

In May 198X, the management team began to work together to develop a framework for strategic planning for XYZ Industries, Inc. Our first objective was to identify the strengths and weaknesses of the corporation. The following were developed during these sessions:

B.   Strengths and Weaknesses

Strengths: Strong, aggressive management team.

Good reputation for quality and service.

Good financial position.

Diversified manufacturing capacity, with technically sound state-of-the-art knowledge and equipment.

Developing emphasis on engineering new products.

<u>Weaknesses</u>: No long-range plan.

Lack of management depth, with little or no management development process.

Sales heavily weighted towards a few big products and customers.

Sales staff technically competent but not professional salesmen.

No formal mechanism for collecting technological or market intelligence.

Customers can perform XYZ's services in-house, which requires continued investment to keep pace with the state of the art.

C. <u>Key Problems and Opportunities</u>

As part of our strategic planning exercise, the XYZ management group reviewed in depth the total operation of the Corporation in order to determine some of our basic problems and the basic opportunities which we should address in the future. It was on this information that we based much of our strategic planning.

<u>Problems</u>:

Training and development of sales personnel.	Requires specific programs, projects, and an implementation schedule. "Sales" personnel versus "service" personnel.
Sales volume increase to cover manufacturing overhead.	At our key manufacturing facilities, unabsorbed overhead creates poor operating performance.
Management Development.	Succession planning and managerial depth are critical to future growth.
Technology.	Constant emphasis is required to remain competitive with our customers, as well as with competitors.

Management Information.   Upgrading and better utilization of data processing information as a management tool is necessary.

Opportunities:

Industrial Coatings.   Appear to have a wide variety of applications for new business at high profit margins.

Electronic Processing.   Increase Engraving Group efficiency and cost effectiveness, and act as a new marketing tool to create new business.

Technological Break-throughs.   Continued R & D and evaluation of marketing plans when they are appropriate for:

         1.   Product
         2.   ”
         3.   ”
         4.   ”
         5.   ”

Color Separations.   Increased penetration and new business development in areas unrelated to commercial printers.

XXXXX^{TM} *Process.*   Licensing sales potential.

D.   General Strategies

After the development of the strengths and weaknesses, the management team developed the following general corporate strategies for 198X:

     1.   Develop marketing plans for 198X for those existing products deemed viable to increase sales and penetration. Specifically, diversification in color separation which should lead to the acquisition of a four-color press at some future date.
     2.   Review and develop a total sales organization, which will: encompass sales training techniques and incentives designed

to improve productivity; measure performance; upgrade the entire selling effort; and collect meaningful usable market and technological intelligence. New Vice-President/Marketing to be in place to accomplish.

3. Develop a marketing plan for the Industrial Coatings utilizing the XXXXX ^{TM} process; said plan to include sales projections for 198X.

4. Develop a plan to promote and evaluate the new electronic process both as a marketing and a production tool.

5. Develop a plan for the creation and operation of a Wallcovering Division within the framework of the ABC Division, to produce, sell, and service previous wallcovering accounts. Develop wallcoverings into a marketable and profitable product line.

6. Develop a marketing plan for the new Packaging Division which will include sales projections for 198X, organizational charts related to its operation, and plans for production and sale of a top quality product.

7. Develop a marketing plan for DEF rolls, including technological innovations, and one which will require market penetration programs and a sales projection for 198X.

8. Develop a marketing plan for licensing of the XXXXX ^{TM} process and sale of coated cylinders.

9. Develop the "conceptual" plan for plastic cylinders, which will require a research budget projection for 198X and the outline of a marketing plan for late 198X or 198X market introduction.

10. Develop a time-phased plan for upgrading the existing MIS capacity to incorporate: the ability to estimate costs for quoting purposes based upon historical experience; inventory control; and more flexible marketing analysis and ability to manage corporate and divisional mailing lists.

11. Develop a management development plan which encompasses: the identification of successsion management for middle-managers; training programs for middle-managers and supervisors designed to upgrade their management skills; cross-pollination of managers for better overall depth of management; and personnel policies and procedures documentation, where necessary.

We expect the implementation of these strategies to bring about a major change in direction for XYZ Industries in the form of creating a change in the delivery system for XYZ's basic products, and exploring new technology that is essential to maintain and gain the competitive advantage in the markets that XYZ serves, with the potential to create new markets. In addition, we will establish a planning discipline that will keep ever-present the key corporate strategies, and a process of evaluating these strategies which will keep the company technologically superior to its competitors, and positioned to take optimum advantage of business opportunities. We are also confident that this process will improve the overall depth of management, marketing, and strategic planning for the future.

About the Plan. . .

It should be noted that one individual is assigned the "ultimate responsibility" for overseeing each strategy. Within the framework of the strategy, other individuals are assigned specific jobs. Again, within the framework of the strategy, these individuals assigned "working responsibilities" basically come under the jurisdiction of the individual assigned with the "ultimate responsibility." A critical part of each of these strategies is the date by which specific functions are to have been completed. All strategies are reviewed at least on a quarterly basis.

These plans were composed jointly by XYZ's top management team and have been reviewed thoroughly with all management and other involved personnel.

A typical strategy from XYZ's Operating Plan:

Personnel Policies and Development

Summary and Objectives

This is a twofold strategy: (1) to develop, standardize wherever possible, and disseminate in a clear and orderly fashion to all personnel, policies and descriptions of company benefits that apply to them as XYZ employees; (2) to develop and assist in the development of all personnel whether it be in operator or management skills so as to continually improve the XYZ "personnel product" and insure timely management and key employee succession.

STRATEGIC MILESTONES

Year	Strategy	Completion Date	Working Responsibility	Estimated Cost to Accomplish
1982	1. Review personnel benefits of all divisions with emphasis on improvement, standardization, and cost savings. Make written recommendations to corporate president to include costs, justification, details, and other pertinent information.	1st Quarter	Personnel Administrator	
	2. List management and key personnel throughout the corporation, including any current or anticipated variances. Determine available back-up from within or, if none available, what outside sources and required actions will be needed to fill requirements. This action will include recruiting, training, and other recommendations. Reports should be in writing and reviewed with other corporate officers for their input.	1st Quarter	President	$5,000
	3. Review with VP/Marketing all sales training plans, including pinpointing potential sales managers and potential sales candidates.	2nd Quarter	President	
	4. Conduct "internal audit" at divisional level to insure personnel policies are being adhered to. Submit report to Group VP and corporate president outlining any and all variations from these policies with the request for corrective action to be taken immediately.	2nd Quarter	Personnel Administrator	

Year	Strategy	Completion Date	Working Responsibility	Estimated Cost to Accomplish
	Responses to be received in writing from Group VP and divisional management.	3rd Quarter	Personnel	
1983	Consideration and investigation of in-house training programs.	2nd Quarter	President	$8,000
	Full-scale personnel manager appointed, with continuation, formalization, and expansion of above policies.	3rd Qaurter	President	$5,000
	Employer survey to be reviewed, revised, and implemented.	3rd Quarter	Personnel	$1,000

On the average it takes about seven full days over at least several months with lots of discussion (even some argument) amongst the management team to reach this point.   Then there are probably three or four more days in between the meetings and at the end to summarize, write, and put the strategic/operating plan document together. What has been accomplished?

- Specific and quantified business objectives.
- A time frame for achieving these objectives.
- Specific strategies that have been time-phased (milestones) and priced-out (capital expenditures).
- Contingency plans for dealing with better than or worse than planned performance.
- The management team's clearer understanding of their working relationships and the need for continued and close cooperation.

You know where you are, where you want to go, and most importantly, how you are going to get there. In addition, you have set in motion a planning discipline and system which will increase your ability to create and control the future of your business.

3
How to Control the Plan

Strategic planning is a two-phased process. Phase I is developing the plan as was discussed in Chapter 2. Phase II involves controlling the plan to make sure that it happens, or more importantly, to insure that the planning process continues to enhance management's ability to continually improve their business planning techniques and results.

COMMITMENT

To accomplish this, management must be committed to: establishing and maintaining the planning discipline; being totally involved all the time; talking about the plan every day; and focusing constantly on planning issues. Commitment by all levels, not just top management, is essential for the development and execution of strategic planning. The ultimate responsibility of the CEO is to see that all levels of management support the plan.

Strategic planning requires changing the way management has thought historically. That doesn't mean to say that day-to-day business management responsibilities will change overnight, but the focus of those daily management activities should change from a present-oriented to a more futuristic concentration. To accomplish this involves sharing the plan with lower levels of management so that they can participate in making the plan happen and can share in the commitment. Likewise, their performance has to be measured against the standards set by the planning process. The only way that these managers can participate is by understanding what strategic planning is all about. This requires senior management explaining that strategic planning is a way to define: the company's purpose in being; their perception of the current and future mix of products; and the qualitative and quantitative projection (short- and long-term) of the total business into the future. It is important to set the stage for every level of management involved in making the plan happen so that they will understand how their function fits into the overall allocation of resources related to the plan.

The commitment issue usually turns out to be a one-time change in philosophy and operating style on the part of management, because once the plan is established and becomes operational, it is adopted as the new standard operating procedure.

Strategic management, this concept of commitment, involves all of the activities of implementation, control, recycling, and reformulating strategies after each planning cycle. Implementation and control are the operational aspects of strategy making. Control is measuring the strategic planning assumptions against actual market conditions and changing trends and patterns in the overall competitive environment.

Business strategy making is a commitment to a management concept that represents a systematic approach to solving complex business problems. For most managers, strategy making and strategic management require adopting a new discipline: one that is attuned to creative and conceptual thinking combined with an almost fervent devotion to the total management of the business from this new strategic perspective.

MUST HAVE A WRITTEN DOCUMENT

All plans have to be in writing for all the reasons mentioned earlier, plus, the written work establishes a clear commitment. The written plan outlines and specifies goals and objectives by function and manager. It puts the words to the numbers and marries both to a responsible manager. It eliminates the misconceptions and misperceptions that permeate an unplanned business environment where nothing is written and no one committed. Good strategies specify who does what, when, and how. Written plans should clearly state:

By Project (Strategy)
What it is we are doing.
Why we are doing it.
Who is responsible for making it happen.

How long it is supposed to take.

How much it has been estimated to cost.

What the expected return is, and how we are going to measure results.

In addition, each strategy is time-phased, usually on a quarterly basis, with specific strategic milestones that have to be monitored. In other words, if there is a strategy that has an 18-month total implementation time, then at 3-month intervals there should be a specific written activities checklist quantifying what has to be accomplished to achieve the overall strategy for each 3-month (quarterly) period.

So the written plan is the guide, and should set the parameters for managing the business. Nothing should be done outside of those parameters because that would be changing the plan. In unplanned businesses, one of the biggest problems is what to do next, and maybe we should try this or that. Each one of those unplanned excursions into this or that dilutes management time, always costs something, and generally tends to weaken the main business of the company. In a planned environment, only those projects that have been thoroughly analyzed and become a part of the written plan are exercised. This is the focusing concept discussed earlier.

These written plans provide management with a chronological perspective of the present and the future. In addition, written plans aid in organizing and administering strategic management, as well as in reconciling personal values among top management, and setting forth broad policies. Written plans really represent a detailed guideline for strategic actions within a time frame.

MUST HAVE FREQUENT PERFORMANCE REVIEWS

One benefit of written time-phased plans is that they set the stage for periodic performance reviews of managers and their strategic milestones by the CEO and by their subordinate managers. This is the essence of the control process. These performance reviews should be monthly and quarterly, and are discussed in detail in Chapter 7.

The performance reviews fine tune the planning process by bringing to the surface basic cause and effect questions, like: How come?;

What are you going to do now?; Why wasn't that considered when the plan was put together?; Why is it going to cost more than was projected?; and How does that affect our contingency plans? Without these frequent scheduled reviews it is difficult to maintain the planning discipline and create the organizational climate absolutely necessary to optimize the strategic planning concept. It is also the only way to achieve a well-balanced appraisal of both the managers and the plan.

Some of the best plans have floundered because there was no concentrated follow-up. Periodic review is not only important for projects that are falling behind plan, but also for projects that are on-target, and those ahead of plan, so that all of these situations can be taken into consideration and measured against the total company plan. Management has to be able to assess where to continue to allocate and reallocate resources, and when to exercise contingency plans. As with all things in business and life, some projects are more successful than others, and the repetitive nature of the planning process is designed to incorporate these successes and failures into planning for the future.

MUST UPDATE STRATEGIES AND PLAN ANNUALLY

The point of a continuous planning process is to maintain momentum towards achieving long-range strategic objectives. This means that some of the strategies initially conceived will change, some will be aborted, and new strategies conceived as time progresses, with management measuring their progress towards the overall mission. This continuous process of evaluation, analysis, and revision is part of the dynamic nature of planning.

The first step in the performance review phase is the quarterly review. The quarterly evaluation of performance against strategic milestones produces these changes in strategies, and the consequent reallocation of resources, quarter by quarter. Management's ability to make the plan happen, or not happen, results in the reformulation of plans. The planning cycle is an annual event wherein the short-range strategies are modified based on the experience from last year, and new strategies are developed to continue the overall momentum towards the ultimate goals of the strategic plan. The quarterly reviews are the interim strategic review steps between annual planning cycles.

It is important to recognize that the annual planning cycle is not another total strategic planning exercise, but rather an opportunity to review levels of success and failure with current strategies to decide on how to continue with or alter those plans, and to agree on what else has to be done in the next operating planning period to continue towards the strategic plan objectives. During the annual planning cycle, management reviews all of their options, changes in the marketplace since the last cycle, technology advances, and progress on strategies underway. It is their chance to match the experience gained from trying to implement strategies with the planning assumptions made for those strategies, and create new plans that have a greater chance of success, as the planning exercise becomes more effective. The planning cycle period is an opportunity for the management team to review plans for the base business as well as strategies developed for future growth.

Understanding the control aspects tends to be one of the most difficult tasks for managers first starting out in strategic planning. This is because you are trying to get people reprogrammed from short-term to long-term thinking. As has been and will continue to be emphasized, this is not an easy task. You are basically forcing managers to form their own realistic performance evaluation system – one which requires them to submit written planning assumptions for the company's future. When you consider that most managers don't have a career plan for *themselves,* this kind of planning for the future is completely foreign to them.

So control really turns out to be a strategic management issue that seeks to insure that performance conforms to plans. Management control involves evaluating the performance of individual managers in making their strategies happen, and taking corrective action when performance varies from plans. In the planning process, there is a continuous narrowing of detail from broad strategic goals to very specific time-phased tactics. These specific strategies require good performance standards and continuous appraisal.

Good performance standards should be built into the management information system, and should be part of the key performance indicators that management uses to monitor the business. Obviously, these kinds of control reports will vary in detail, depending upon the different levels of management that are monitoring plans within the organization. Setting standards for planning assumptions is another new challenge for managers who are new to the planning process.

This measurement of past performance, and the projections that good managers should be able to make from the ongoing review of plan-to-actual, should make management more sensitive and alert to what is going on or is likely to happen to their business. Designing an effective system of controls takes time, and starts with management. Management has to be able to sort out and deal with the fact that there is a difference between strategic management and operational management. Strategic management is done by those at the top of the organization, and everything else is operational management. However, strategic and operational management are closely interrelated. Strategic management provides the direction and parameters for operational management. It is the process of managing the mission after it has been determined what the business is, and how management will direct the organization through the operational objectives that have been developed into specific strategies that represent today's decisions to achieve tomorrow's results. Peter Drucker captured this concept aptly in his often quoted axiom: "Planning and doing are separate parts of the same job; they are not separate jobs."

The key to good control is developing good operating plans and budgets. The operating plan, of which the budget is the first year, is the method of integrating strategic plans into current goals, objectives, and standards for coordinating activities that provide a basis for controlling performance to see that it is in conformance with the plan. The operating plan represents the linkage with the strategic plan and is the vehicle that lends operating credibility to planning. The budget really functions to convert the planned objectives into quantitative goals that can be coordinated with the different functional operations of the company. Operating plans translate strategic decisions into action plans. Chapter 4 deals with these issues of integration, linkage, and translation.

4
How Strategic Plans and Budgets Interface

As was discussed in Chapters 2 and 3, the strategic plan identifies what has to be done with the existing business to establish a sound base from which to launch more futuristic plans. In practice, the strategic plan sets a conceptual set of future goals and works back in time to the operating plan via the time-phased strategies in the strategic plan.

OPERATING PLANS EXPLAINED

Operating plans are usually three years long, including the budget (the first year). They are more specific than strategic plans. Operating plans quantify the first three years of the strategic plan. They specify how the base business will grow, product by product, and how strategies will foster the incremental growth of the base business with new products, or by-products.

Operating plans outline this growth process year by year, and identify capital expenditures and human resource requirements annually. The annual plans are also broken down by quarter so that each phase of growth can be planned and projected clearly. In this way, management has plotted the course of the business and can see the task they have set out for themselves.

More importantly, the trade-offs are obvious, and the alternatives have a price tag that can be assessed in light of changing conditions in the marketplace.

It is also important to use the operating plan as a basis for assessing management's ability to plan consistently. One way that this is accomplished is by comparing the plans made for a given year in one operating plan to the plans made for that same year in the next operating plan. This is another technique that is utilized to improve the planning process constantly. The basic question to be asked is, "What are the differences in the planning assumptions between those developed last year for next year and those developed this year for next year, and why?"

THE BUDGET AS PART OF THE OPERATING PLAN

As has been stated earlier, the budget constitutes the first year of the operating plan. The budget is the most detailed part of the entire planning process, because it requires month-by-month quantification of every aspect of the business. Budgeting is the process of establishing revenue and expense objectives for all elements of the firm. The budget is where the base business is integrated with the strategies to produce a projection of the total business plans for one (the next) year.

The budget takes the most recent actual experience and uses it as the basis for analyzing how the next year will be projected, taking into consideration the success or failure of current strategies. The budget fixes responsibilities for short-term performance and identifies strategic milestones for the purpose of planning management compensation. The budget is the base point for the rest of the operating plan.

The out years of the operating plan are projected off of the budget year assumptions, and from the implementation of strategies that span the operating plan period, some of which: start and end in the budget year; conclude in the budget year from a prior year; start in the budget year and continue/conclude in the out years; or, start in the out years and continue/conclude in the out years. When done well, one operating plan flows into another with a well-coordinated updating. However, when first starting out on the strategic planning experience, it will probably take several tries to accomplish a smooth integration from one operating plan to the next.

When the planning process is functioning properly, strategies will be critiqued continuously, and management will maintain an objective perspective on what they really are trying to accomplish. With just annual budgets, there is a general tendency to continue to pursue plans that management wants to come true, rather than a more realistic longer-term outlook with strategic milestones that give managers the option to reallocate resources based upon what they have actually been able to accomplish, and what they haven't. Annual budgets just give managers a change to "try again next year."

THE BUDGET AS THE FIRST PART OF THE STRATEGIC PLAN

The result of the initial strategic planning exercise is that the operating plan usually becomes the first operating plan that the company has had, and replaces what was called the long-range plan, if they had one. In this case, the budget is a very significant part of the strategic plan because it represents the initial quantification of strategies, and the first attempt on the part of management to think strategically. It is also the first time that management is trying to manage strategies that go out beyond the annual plan. The key word here is "manage" because most long-range plans are just extrapolations of the current year into the future – not real attempts at analyzing alternatives each step of the way. They also contain no contingency plans to deal with "What do we do if we don't accomplish the plan?"

Strategic management requires a basic change in the way the management team works together, and works for the CEO. Initially a somewhat uncomfortable, different kind of commitment beyond the management-by-objective (MBO) techniques of old has to be established, because it is the first time you are asking your managers to step out of their comfortable operations-oriented mode into a sort of brave new world of contingency plans and really futuristic thinking. Just using the word "strategy" implies something beyond next month, quarter, or year.

So, getting the first operating plan put together is usually quite a task. The key to the task is rearranging the old budget, and "stretching" it out two more years. Rearranging it isn't too hard, but stretching it out is tough. To have a real planning environment, management must be sure it is not just "projecting the now," but rather that it is asking the right tough questions about the future. Strategic change cannot be accomplished in a year. It follows then that good planning requires a commitment of management resources in terms of innovation, intuitive thinking, and market intelligence beyond those needed for budgeting.

Every book on management preaches that planning should precede budgeting. This fundamental concept is that any objective setting should take place only after the future direction of the business has been established, and resources committed, to ensure the future viability of the firm. This involves dealing with many more unknowns than in simple budgeting. It is more difficult and much more complicated to quantify several years of the future — in terms of the product mix, the competition, and the external environment — rather than just one year.

The budget contains the strategies that have been identified as necessary to effect the trade-offs between current and future profits. The budget is that clearly defined linkage between strategic plans and operating plans. It represents the only way that management can see the balance that the planning process establishes between the present and future needs of the business. The budgeting-operating planning cycle is the only process that allows this balancing mechanism to work effectively. We are all aware, from the past, that without a balancing mechanism, the current short-term prospects will continue to dominate the planning process, with all of the attendant excuses for why managers couldn't see what was going to happen (because they weren't looking).

Without a good linkage between planning and budgeting, managers will continue to make those easier, more comfortable, short-term operating decisions. If you don't change the managers' incentive by building into the budget a compensation plan for accomplishing the key strategic milestones for current and future strategies, there is no reason for the managers to make any other than short-term decisions, because that is what they think they are paid to do.

Let's review what we have done so far in the strategic planning initial exercise, and how that fits in with operating plans and budgets.

1. We evaluated the strengths and weaknesses and agreed upon what they are.
2. We developed strategies to:

2. a. Solidify our base business and continue to grow the best part of it with viable plans we are convinced will work.
    b. Get out of marginally profitable products or market segments where we will never be able to do any better than we have, historically.
    c. Stop diluting our time and effort exploring concepts and new products that are unrelated to the basic nature of our business.
    d. Explore by-products of our existing products and cost-effective technological innovations to improve market share and profitability.
    e. Explore only new business opportunities where there is some synergy with our existing know-how, channels of distribution, and management talents.
    f. Invest in continuous management development, training, and cross-pollination of our human resources.
3. We priced-out and time-phased these strategies, and assigned responsibilities to respective managers.
4. We prepared our initial mission statement to set parameters for what we want to do and be.

Now we have to take the product of that effort and fold it into our "old" way of budgeting, and then extend it into the replacement for the long-range plan, called the operating plan. Ideally, operating plans should allow management to go from the very specific month-by-month details of the budget year into the future of the next few years with lessening detail, but with clear parameters in regard to the strategic direction of the business. In other words, the budget contains the units, prices, quantities, costs, and expense details of our current product mix. The next year of the operating plan is produced by adding our best estimate of this year's mix to the expected results of planned strategies to alter that mix, volume, or market share. The third year of the operating plan is a projection of this year's mix with the anticipated trade-offs in products and profits planned for the first two years. It is important to realize that when operating plans are developed they contain the best thinking at that time about the anticipated results of well-thought-out strategies.

The entire planning process is designed to encourage this kind of systematic thinking ahead by management, to:

1. Get managers to be better prepared for sudden new developments that can be either favorable or unfavorable.
2. Give managers a more vivid sensitivity toward their interacting responsibilities.
3. Increase and extend the overall goals and objectives of the company.
4. Better coordinate the efforts of management, the utilization of resources, and the development of performance standards for control.

So the real secret to success in integrating strategic planning with operating plans and budgets is the level of management talent available to overlay the strategic plan on the organization effectively.

Figure 4.1 captures the integration of the strategic plan with the operating plan and highlights the time frames associated with the strategic plan (five years), the operating plan (three years), and the first year of the plan – the budget. It also lists the key components of each phase of the overall plan.

Figure 4.2 is a graphic display of all of the steps discussed thus far in the strategic planning process, and gives a good qualitative overview of what has to happen in each step of the exercise and the critical questions that have to be answered by the management team if they want to have a realistic plan. To summarize:

Where are we (What is our present nature?)?
What do we want to be (What should the character of our company be?)?
How are we going to get there?
What must we do right now?
What progress have we made because we planned it that way?

What we are really trying to overlay on any business through strategic planning is a way to get the management team to sift through all of the elements of their business and sort out the most important, or

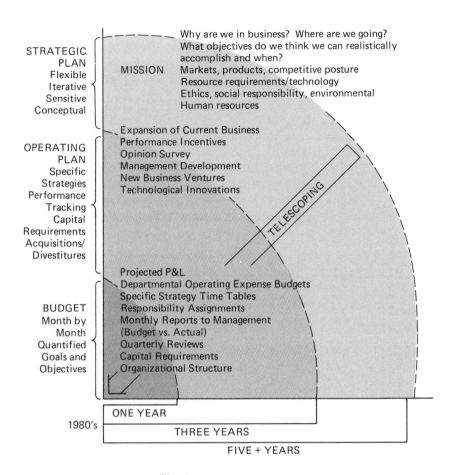

STRATEGIC
PLAN
Flexible
Iterative
Sensitive
Conceptual

MISSION

Why are we in business? Where are we going?
What objectives do we think we can realistically
accomplish and when?
Markets, products, competitive posture
Resource requirements/technology
Ethics, social responsibility, environmental
Human resources

OPERATING
PLAN
Specific
Strategies
Performance
Tracking
Capital
Requirements
Acquisitions/
Divestitures

Expansion of Current Business
Performance Incentives
Opinion Survey
Management Development
New Business Ventures
Technological Innovations

TELESCOPING

BUDGET
Month by
Month
Quantified
Goals and
Objectives

Projected P&L
Departmental Operating Expense Budgets
Specific Strategy Time Tables
Responsibility Assignments
Monthly Reports to Management
(Budget vs. Actual)
Quarterly Reviews
Capital Requirements
Organizational Structure

ONE YEAR

1980's

THREE YEARS

FIVE + YEARS

Fig. 4.1.

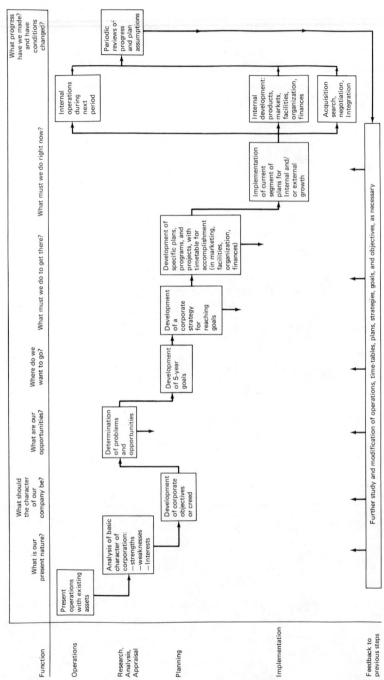

The Process of Strategic Planning

Fig. 4.2.

at least, to return some element of objectivity to day-to-day management. If they can at least accomplish that, then they should have before them an array of opportunities and threats to deal with which, combined with some futuristic thinking and analysis, is the beginning of developing a way to address the key strategic issues that are the secret to balancing the present with the future.

5
How to Develop a Good Budget (Operating Plan)

Budgeting is establishing revenue, expense, and cash flow goals and controls. The parameters for those goals are the strategies for the operating plan discussed earlier.

Most businesses relate all of their planning to the anticipated sales level. Sales forecasting then becomes the first step in the budget preparation process.

SALES PROJECTIONS

Sales projections can be made by considering the following factors:

Historical Experience. Every business has accumulated historical sales data. Most of this data is by product and customer. It then follows that the same customers who have been buying specific products for the last few years probably will buy those products next year. So the level of sales attributable to those customers, under normal conditions, can be expected to recur next year. You can also survey your customers and get some idea of their buying intentions for next year. The simplest way to project historical sales is to list all of your customers, what they have bought over the last few years, and then project what you expect them to buy next year (Exhibit 5.1). Then ask them to verify how realistic they think that is.

In addition, every year you have had some sales from new customers. You should be able to track that new business historically, and project at least the average from over the last few years as anticipated sales from new customers for next year.

Statistics. Trends and patterns are natural by-products of being in business. Things like average increases in sales by product can be

Exhibit 5.1 Key Market Segment.

XYZ Company

PRODUCTS BY RANK	KEY CUSTOMERS BY RANK	SALES (Obj.) (x $000)
1	ABC CO.	$ 350,000
	DEF CO.	310,000
2	GHI CO.	295,000
	JKL CO.	260,000
3	M CO.	215,000
	N CO.	165,000
4	OP CO.	430,000
	QR CO.	370,000
	S CO.	250,000
	T CO.	195,000
	UV CO.	325,000
	X CO.	285,000
		192,000
	YZ CO.	521,000
	CBA CO.	470,000
	FED CO.	390,000
	IHG CO.	325,000
	J CO.	265,000

tracked, and if the time period being analyzed is long enough to trace a trend of pattern, that trend, in most cases, is likely to continue. Likewise, relationships between products (the effect that the sales of one has on another) produce patterns. These kinds of product mix factors are important for planning.

It is also possible to take your sales data and statistically compare it to any number of economic indicators. The statistical comparisons can take the form of correlation or regression analysis, which reveals if product sales data lead, or lag, a specific economic indicator. If a statistically significant pattern is discernible, then it can be used for planning future sales projections. By tracking those economic indicators and getting the projections for the indicators, you can use this information to better plan for the sales projections for your products.

Statistical techniques and models are important budgeting tools that have application throughout the budget preparation process which will be discussed throughout this book.

Known Events.   New product introductions, price increases, and product deletions also have to be factored into the sales projection, and time-phased. Known events and anticipated actions by competitors should also be planned for in any sales projection.

Pricing exercises (increases and decreases) are another very important aspect of sales planning, as is the time-phasing of price changes. Known events also relate to manpower changes, capital expenditures, and all other aspects of budgeting for your business.

Economy.   Almost every business reacts to the economy in some way. Future projections about the economy in a macro sense have to be considered in developing any sales projection.

In addition, your industry may have its own trade association that refines the overall economic projection, which is an added feature to consider.

The way that budgets are spread by month is usually heavily impacted by economic forecasts.

Intuitive Feel of Management.   In all businesses, even after the most sophisticated techniques have been used to develop the sales projection, management usually makes adjustments based upon experience. They do this by the application of their "intuition" after seeing the final projection. An example might be a senior executive looking at the numbers and saying, "I understand the logic that went into developing the projection, but I just don't think that will happen, and this (the swift stroke of a pencil) is a sales level that I feel more comfortable with, and I think will really happen."

Most sales projections are developed by the marketing staff, but should be shared with the sales force for their input, as they have to make it happen. In the case of sales by customer, the sales force can usually provide that information. One of the best ways to fine tune sales projecting is to have the sales force develop their best estimate by product and by customer, independent of the marketing staff, and then to compare the two. The results of these kinds of discussions usually make for a more realistic projection than taking just one or the other.

In the process of developing the sales projection, and considering all of these factors, there are usually several sets of numbers that result from various price and volume assumptions. These sets of numbers are the basis for developing contingency plans, discussed later in the book.

MANUFACTURING BUDGETS

Once the sales projection has been finalized, forecasting of manufacturing cost can begin.

The process starts with the product-by-product sales projection given to the manufacturing staff. The major reason for this is to make sure that the production facilities have the capacity to produce the forecast, and more importantly, to allow them to figure out how much it will cost to make all of the products projected to be sold next year — product by product.

The manufacturing costing process is a three-part exercise made up of:

Raw Materials Planning. In most companies, each product the company makes has a different mix of materials in its makeup. All of these materials have individual costs which must be considered and planned for. Each of these materials may have fluctuating costs which must also be considered.

Raw materials planning is the process of estimating, by product, how much of each material will be needed to make all of the products projected to be sold, projecting the cost of those materials, and time-phasing the purchase and use of each material.

Direct Labor Planning. The workers who put the products together are considered direct labor, for costing purposes. Each step in the process of making every product requires some direct labor input. Direct labor costing is estimating how much time each step in the manufacturing process will take for each product, and then costing that out based upon the product, and the labor rate per worker, per step.

The direct labor estimate is then calculated for all of the products in the sales projection.

Overhead Planning.   All of the other employees who work at the manufacturing facility, but are not directly involved in the making of the products, are usually referred to as indirect labor. These people (their salaries and benefits) and any other costs related to them, and all of the other costs (depreciation of the plant and everything in it, utilities, maintenance, security insurance, real estate taxes, etc.) associated with running the manufacturing facility, are usually called manufacturing "overhead." This overhead must also be estimated, taking into consideration inflation, and allocated to all the products projected to be made next year. Each overhead item has to have its own basis for allocation to individual products, and is an exercise unto itself.

So, projecting the manufacturing cost budget is taking the sales projection and estimating all of the components (materials, labor, and overhead) that make up manufacturing cost, by product. This then becomes what is commonly referred to as the manufacturing budget. Manufacturing manpower needs are also developed in this exercise, as well as capital expenditures planned for manufacturing purposes.

EXPENSE BUDGETS

Once the sales projection and manufacturing cost projection have been completed and management has a gross profit estimate, operating expenses can then be developed.

Operating expenses are all the monies associated with marketing and administering the company, as well as any monies planned for research and development. Expense budgeting is the process by which the departmental managers estimate their respective departmental operating expenses for the next year. Expense budgets are usually developed by department, within function. Departmental expenses encompass things like: compensation, benefits, telephone, travel, office supplies, publications, corporate overhead allocations, and whatever other expenses are peculiar to each respective department. Most departmental expenses can be projected from historical experience and factored for growth, decline, and/or inflation.

Department managers use the company guidelines on compensation and inflation factors in combination with historical experience for estimating most operating expenses. Obviously, employee additions and terminations have to be time-phased, and any major variances from the current year's projected expenses should be explained. Manpower budgets are also a by-product of this exercise.

Once the schedule of expenses has been developed, the company pro forma profit and loss statement (Sales, less cost and expenses) can be estimated for next year's budget. At this point in the budget development process, from examining the numbers, it should be clear whether or not the company financial guidelines have been adhered to, and the profit objectives and growth criteria achieved. Throughout the process, senior management should be monitoring the development of the budget and making sure that realistic and achievable estimates are being made. This is easily done from observation of historical experience.

After the pro forma profit and loss statement has been tentatively approved by management, the balance sheet and other key financial ratios can be developed. This is the process of developing the data for the asset management section of the budget. Cash and receivables balances are calculated from the year-end estimates and the budget projections. Likewise, ending inventory and other asset balances are also calculated. Liabilities are projected from the year-end estimated balances and the budget data for next year. There is no standardized format for the asset management section, and every company tends to develop formats for the kinds of financial presentations that suit the nature of their business. The most important element in preparing the asset management section is developing the key financial indicators that were referred to above. These should be displayed in a way that highlights the most significant financial aspects of the business. In most cases, these have to do with cash flow and return on assets.

While the majority of this discussion has concentrated on the budget, we are really talking about the budget as part of the operating plan. In Chapter 4, we discussed the fact that the budget is the first year of the operating plan, and that the budget is the most detailed part of the entire planning process. We also said that the budget is the base point for the rest of the operating plan.

Once the budget data is approved by management, the *out* years (next two) of the operating plan can be developed. Again, operating plans evolve out of the strategic planning process, and represent the best effort at quantifying the expected results of the strategies planned to be implemented during the operating plan period, as well as those underway from earlier operating plans, and some that may continue beyond the current operating plan. The exercise of quantifying all of these futuristic plans is very challenging to the management team just starting out in planning. It is especially difficult for those who haven't even looked that far ahead in their personal lives.

In any case, developing projections for the out years is a combination of estimating the growth, or change, in the base business off of what is in the budget year, and supplementing that with anticipated results of strategies implemented in the budget year for those years. A company's ability to forecast the out years off of the budget year is a function of the nature of their business and the length of time they have been in business. For most firms, projecting the shape of their base business for the out years should be achievable without too much difficulty, assuming sufficient time and analysis have already been put into the planning process.

The only data that has to be added to the projection of the base business to complete the operating plan is, new or increased business expected from new strategies planned to be implemented in the out years. Here again, if the right analysis was done during the planning process, these numbers should also be readily available.

An important point to remember is that the budget year detail is very specific, but the out years detail is usually less specific. In the out years, the expectation should be that you are trying to achieve reasonably reliable orders of magnitude. While in the budget year, the projections have to be the best estimate of every aspect of the business. The out years detail for sales and profits is usually estimated strategy by strategy, and quantified in the capital expenditures section of the overall operating plan.

CAPITAL EXPENDITURES BUDGETS

The last data developed is the capital expenditures budget. Capital expenditures are the monies projected to be spent on major investment projects that are related to cost savings or business expansion programs, and that have identifiable strategies.

In most companies there is a capital expenditure policy, and there are procedures to be followed in developing capital expenditure requests. It is important to develop capital expenditure proposals as far in advance as possible so that "approval-in-principle" can be obtained from company management, before developing all of the required supplementary analysis. If strategic planning is functioning properly, this will be a natural by-product of that process.

Each capital expenditure program requires return-on-investment (ROI) justification, which is determined by company management. Capital expenditures are usually projected by quarter, for cash planning purposes, as well as for the evaluation of strategic milestones. So the total capital expenditures budget is broken down into quarters, and projected over the life of each project. In addition, projects are usually categorized by the dollar value to be invested in each category of expenditure (i.e., over or under $100,000, $250,000, or $500,000 of total expenditures). There is also usually a miscellaneous category for the routine replacement of assets under a certain amount of money per asset type.

The quarterly projection of capital expenditures is usually part of the asset management section of the operating plan. Those projects that have been approved by management are separated from those that are being submitted for approval-in-principle. The operating plan review presents a good opportunity for corporate management to discuss with operating management the projects submitted for approval-in-principle.

CONTINGENCY PLANNING

To assume that the plan will work as planned is not good planning. There are always forces at work in the marketplace and in the economy, and mystical factors having to do with luck, fate, and technological breakthroughs at the most unexpected times. The acceptance of these facts of life and business has created the need to have contingency plans. In addition, good management requires exploring alternatives and developing a way to deal with all of the what-ifs that could possibly happen.

Contingency planning is another aspect of good budgeting, and sometimes is also referred to as flexible budgeting. Most contingency plans are based upon a range of forecasts of less than and more than budgeted volumes. When the sales projections that were referred to at the beginning of the chapter are being developed, there are usually a number of assumptions that go into coming up with the best estimate. These assumptions, or the answers to the what-if questions, are also the basis for the decisions that ultimately make up the contingency plans.

An easy way to think about contingency plans is to use the "BOP" approach, where:

B – stands for the BEST estimate, the Plan, or the Budget data.
O – represents the OPTIMISTIC projection, assuming that everything is favorable and all of our plans work better than expected, and budgeted.
P – means PESSIMISTIC, assuming the worst of all of the what-if scenarios.

Of course there can be a variety contingency plans that range from the worst case to the best case to the most optimistic, but for purposes of illustration, the B-O-P explanation is the easiest to understand when first starting out in planning. To carry this just one step further, an example of how contingency plans could be presented as part of the budget would be:

Case:	I	II	III	IV	V	–or–	B	O	P
Sales									
Cost of Sales									
Gross Profit									
Expenses									
Net Profit									
Assumptions									

Besides demonstrating that you are a good planner by having developed these contingency plans in the first place, the real value of the exercise is:

1. You realize the need to plan for, and appreciate more, the concept of *what-if* this really does happen.
2. You have analyzed and developed well-thought-out ways to deal with these potential contingencies so that you will not get caught by surprise and revert to your old crisis management style when they actually happen.
3. You are starting to act and think like a planner by creating a full range of future possibilities on paper.

Contingency planning also requires setting up a new tracking mechanism called key performance, or trend, indicators, which are discussed in more detail in chapter 7. Basically, these trend indicators are used in conjunction with a concept called trigger points which represent predetermined levels in the trend at which one of the contingency plans would be exercised. To illustrate:

TRENDS, TREND INDICATORS, TRIGGER POINTS

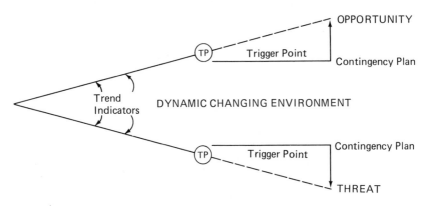

Trends: When you can connect two or more points to show a direction.
Trend Indicators: The quantifiable, factual data ($, units, ratios, costs, pounds, margins, shipments, etc.) that can be tracked to monitor your trend (favorable/unfavorable).
Trigger Point: The predetermined level that will cause you to exercise one of your contingency plans.

6
What Does a Good Budget Look Like?

To most managers who have never planned well before, just getting all the numbers together is quite an accomplishment. However, the numbers only have meaning if you are intimately familiar with how they were calculated, and usually, subordinate managers only develop budget data for their areas of responsibility. To breathe life into the budget you need to marry a narrative to the numbers so that the total budget has meaning to every manager.

FORMAT

The format for the budget document should be made up of the following sequence of sections:

Summary and Highlights. This section should be an introduction to the plan, summarizing this year's expected results as compared to this year's budget, as well as next year's projected plan compared to this year's anticipated results. Highlights of major events — in the marketplace, with competitors, and with the economy, should also be discussed in this section. The summary and highlights section should be one to two pages in length.

Key Problems and Opportunities. This section is a listing of, first, problems with which management must deal in the upcoming year, and then, opportunities that can be exploited. It is important to explore these issues because it fosters creative thinking, which is the essence of good planning. It is also important to distinguish between key problems and operational routine problems. An example of a key problem would be: "Our inability to produce detailed cost reports by product, which makes product pricing decisions very difficult"; as opposed to: "We need to speed up the process of getting the monthly financial statements." Most often, key problems are related to strategies, either directly or indirectly. The identification of key problems and opportunities creates a checklist for management to use, from one operating plan budget to the next.

Marketing Summary. This section is a product-by-product discussion of markets, market share, pricing, and competitors, supported by product profit and loss statements. It is also good to array all of the product P & Ls on one schedule to illustrate each product's contribution to sales and profits of the total business.

Strategies. The strategies section is one of the most important sections, as it identifies all of the action plans for the coming years, what they are, who is responsible for making them happen, how much each will cost, how long they will take with quarterly milestones, and what is the anticipated return. Strategies are listed strategy by strategy, as illustrated later in this chapter.

Asset Management. This is the financial section that deals with the overall profit and loss, the balance sheet, key financial ratios, and capital expenditures. Cash flow schedules are also part of the asset management section.

Organization. The last section contains the total organization chart for the company, and manpower schedules by department within function for last year, this year, and next year.

This kind of format allows the budget to become more of a story about what's happening in the business rather than just a collection of numbers. To review what is accomplished by having a narrative to support the numbers:

- The summary and highlights section introduces the business circumstances for this year and next year.
- The key problems and opportunities section identifies all of the major challenges facing management.
- The marketing summary details the market position, volume, and profitability of each product.
- The strategies section outlines the major plans that management has developed to deal with the present and the future.

- The asset management section contains all of the relevant financial information about the business.
- The organizational section outlines the structure and manpower.

When well done, a budget written in this format could be given to a newly hired manager, and after reading it from cover to cover, he/she would have a good understanding of the business.

CONTENT BY SECTION

Summary and Highlights

This section is designed as a general introduction to the budget and should contain information pertaining to the anticipated results of this year, like: "Sales for 19XX are projected to be $XXX, which is X% of this year's budget and X% of last year's. Earnings are expected to be $XXX, X% of last year." It should also contain a brief discussion of significant events that happened this year related to products, markets, competitors, and the economy. Some selected commentary from a typical company's summary and highlights would be:

"Sales in 198X were up 14.9%, with earnings up 12.8%. These results were in line with our original plans, and particularly gratifying in view of the economic environment and the fact that we continued to make substantial investments in the future in all four segments of the business.

"We continued to invest heavily in pharmaceutical research, with spending up from $87,000 to $104,000, or 11.9% of our pharmaceutical sales in 198X.

"The extensive reorganization efforts in our domestic hospital and professional businesses have been accomplished with a minimum of disruption, although at somewhat greater expense than anticipated.

"We got out of the needle and syringe business, which was only marginally profitable in 198X, and increased our effort on the higher technology specialty ends of our various hospital businesses.

"While we expect to see some improvements, our diagnostic imaging operations will show substantial losses again in 198X as we continue to invest heavily in research and development.

"In February of this year we announced the cessation of marketing efforts for our disposable diaper line. A year ago we commented that substantial product improvements by competitors, coupled with increased marketing expenditures on their part, had caused us to fall short of our goals. This continued to be the case into 1981 and, consequently, we have decided to redirect those resources elsewhere at this time."

The same presentation should be made for next year's budget data, summarizing the projected change in sales and earnings as compared to the expected results for this year, as well as the highlights of significant plans for next year. Major new capital expenditure projects should also be discussed briefly.

A well-done summary and highlights section usually does not take more than one or two pages.

Key Problems and Opportunities

The identification of problems and opportunities is a reflection of good management. It allows for creative thinking, which results in good planning. Good management doesn't react to problems, it anticipates them. The key problems and opportunities section is a listing of each problem and opportunity, and an explanation of the action plans that have been designed to deal with them.

It is important to be sure to differentiate between normal operating situations and key problems and opportunities. An example of some typical key problems and opportunities is.

Key
Problems:
- We do not have an effective call reporting system for our salesmen.
- We do not have detailed cost information by product.
- Our line of widgets is slowly becoming noncompetitive.

Opportunities:
- The recent price increase by the XYZ Company should allow us to get some of their business.
- The change in policy from using distributors to going to their own sales personnel by the ABC Company should permit us to pick up a few key distributors.

The key problems and opportunities should be the accumulation of all of those suggested by the respective operating managers.

Marketing Summary

This section is a thorough discussion of each product, which usually is accompanied by product profit and loss statements. At either the beginning or the end of the marketing summary, there can be a consolidation company P & L schedule, with the products going across the top, and a total of all the products in the last column.

It is a good way to see an array of all of the products, and each product's contribution to the total sales and earnings.

It is also a good way to force management to concentrate on the performance of each product and to be aware of the role each product plays in the overall projected sales and earnings results of the company.

Price, volume, competition (market share), and future plans for each product should be discussed thoroughly in this section.

An example of how products should be arranged in the marketing summary is:

Marketing Summary

Products	1	2	3	4	5	6	7	TOTAL
Sales								
Cost of Sales								
Gross Profit								
Expenses								
Net Profit								
Assumptions								
Average Price								
Units								
Market Share								

Strategies

This section should include the identification of specific objectives, the rationale for each strategy, the sequential steps that must be taken to achieve the strategic objectives, the assignment of responsibilities, and the setting of target dates (strategic milestones). Strategies are designed to accomplish goals related to supporting sales and income growth during the planning period.

Only major strategies should be included in the final budget document, and each strategy should be condensed into three pages of narrative or less. Each strategy should be self-contained and should not require reference to another section of the plan to make it complete.

This section may also contain discussions of strategies that are being presented to company management for "approval-in-principle." These strategies usually represent major changes in direction, and require analysis and commitment of funds outside of the normal course of the business.

The major strategies included in this section may be new or carried forward from this year's plan. In the order of presentation, new strategies should precede continuing strategies. In addition, a listing of all the major strategies from this year's plan should be included at the end of the strategies section, and whether each one is continuing, has been cancelled, or completed should be indicated. There should be brief explanations of the results of completed strategies, and reasons why cancelled strategies were discontinued.

The format for strategy presentation should be:

Major Strategy No. _____TITLE_____

I. WHAT (is to be accomplished). This should be a brief statement of the strategic objective made simply and explicitly. Quantify material wherever possible. Avoid vague and general explanations.

II. STATUS. New or continuing – and if continuing, a brief progress report should be included.

III. WHY (it is to be accomplished). This should be a rational discussion of what the problem is and/or of the opportunity to be taken, and should clearly state the reasons for the strategy.

IV. HOW (it is to be accomplished). This should be the sequential steps in the plan of action developed to accomplish the WHAT. Alternatives considered should be mentioned in explaining why the action plan was chosen. This requirement can represent a good basis for dialogue with company management.

V. WHO and WHEN (responsibility and timing). This is best accomplished by a table with the column headings *Who* and *When*, listing entries by title and by a specific date, respectively. This makes for a simplified follow-up and control technique. For an example of a typical strategy, please refer back to Chapter 1.

The strategies section is an integral part of the budget, and supports key problems and opportunities, as well as the marketing summary.

Asset Management

The asset management section is the financial section. It contains the overall projected profit and loss statement for the company, key balance sheet data, and important financial ratios. Receivables, inventories, and payables balances are highlighted.

Cash flow schedules should also be part of the asset management section, with appropriate commentary, where that commentary will clarify the numbers.

In addition, there should be a capital expenditures schedule included in the asset management section.

An example of the asset management section would be.

XYZ COMPANY

Asset Management Section

PROFIT AND LOSS		
Operating Period 19X1–X3		
19X1	**19X2**	**19X3**
Sales		
Cost of Sales		
Gross Profit		
Expenses		
Net Profit		

BALANCE SHEET		
Operating Period 19X1–X3		
Assets **19X1**	**19X2**	**19X3**
Cash $	$	$
Accounts Receivable		
Inventory		
Other Assets		
Machinery and Equip-ment (Depreciation)		

Buildings
(Depreciation) _____ _____ _____

   TOTAL ASSETS $ _____ $ _____ $ _____

	19X1	19X2	19X3
Liabilities			
Accounts Payable	$	$	$
Taxes Payable			
Notes Payable			
Loans Payable			
TOTAL LIABILITIES	$ _____	$ _____	$ _____
Stockholders Equity			
Capital Stock	$	$	$
Retained Earnings			
TOTAL EQUITY	$ _____	$ _____	$ _____

SIGNIFICANT FINANCIAL DATA

	19X1	19X2	19X3
Working Capital	$	$	$
Inventory Turns			
Collection Period			
Debt to Equity			
Return on Assets			

CAPITAL EXPENDITURES

	19X1	19X2	19X3
Replacement of Assets	$	$	$
Strategy I			
Strategy II			
Strategy III			

CASH FLOW			
	19X1	**19X2**	**19X3**
Beginning Cash	$ _____	$ _____	$ _____
Sources: Receivables	$	$	$
Sale of Assets	_____	_____	_____
SUBTOTAL	$ _____	$ _____	$ _____
Uses: Materials	$	$	$
Expenses			
Capital Expenditures			
Loan Repayment	_____	_____	_____
SUBTOTAL	$ _____	$ _____	$ _____
Ending Cash	$ _____	$ _____	$ _____
Borrowings	$	$	$
Investments	$	$	$

Organization

The organization section includes the overall organization chart of the company, with schedules of supporting manpower by department, within function.

Like the key problems and opportunities section, the organization section displays the total organization, and makes quite evident the reporting relationships and levels within the managerial hierarchy.

The manpower by function table allows management to see easily, by job title, where manpower has increased or decreased. These schedules usually have footnotes or supporting narrative for any major increases or decreases in personnel.

An example of the organization section would be:

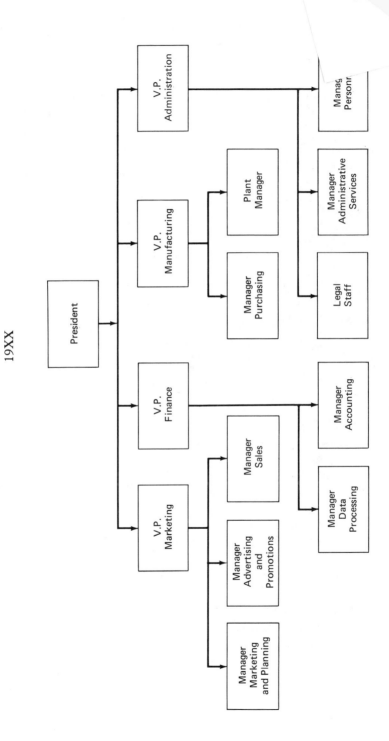

XYZ COMPANY
Organization Chart
19XX

Since manpower makes up a major portion of the expenses of most companies, the organization section is closely scrutinized. Most manpower increases related to increases in business and profits are easily justified, but increases in staff without any directly traceable increase in business, or profits, is difficult to justify.

An example of the Manpower by Function table would be:

MANPOWER BY FUNCTION			
	19X1	19X2	19X3
Office of the President			
CEO			
Secretary			
Staff			
Marketing			
V.P.			
Secretary			
Manager – Planning			
Secretary			
Staff			
Manager – Advertising and Promotions			
Secretary			
Staff			
Manager – Sales			
Secretary			
Field Sales Force			
Region I			
Region II			
Region III			
Distributors			
Region I			
Region II			
Region III			
Finance			
V.P.			
Secretary			
Manager – Data Processing			
Secretary			

	19X1	19X2	19X3
Staff – Analysts			
Programmers			
Operators			
Manager – Accounting			
Secretary			
Staff – Budget Analyst			
Supervisors			
Accounts Supervisor			
Clerks			

Manufacturing
V.P.
Secretary
Assistant
Manager – Purchasing
Secretary
Purchasing Clerks
Manager – Plant
Secretary
Supervisors
Foreman
Workers

Administration
V.P.
Secretary
Legal Staff
Lawyers
Secretary
Clerk
Manager – Administrative Services
Secretary
Clerks
Manager – Personnel
Secretary
Compensation and Benefits Analyst
Interviewers
Clerks

TOTAL PERSONNEL

BENEFITS OF DEVELOPING THE BUDGET DOCUMENT

The benefits of developing the budget document are:

1. It tells the story of the business and has to be logical to make sense to the writer and reader.
2. It highlights variances from the past and requires an explanation of each variance.
3. It forces managers to "think" more about their projections because they have to explain what they've done, in writing.
4. It is a written commitment to a well-thought-out plan.
5. It forms the basis for comparing actual results to the written planning assumptions.
6. It acts as an audit trail for future plans and planning.
7. It sets out every strategy so that each can be scrutinized carefully, and questioned.
8. It identifies problems, and highlights opportunities that can be looked back upon in evaluating managerial performance.
9. It is one of the few ways yet devised to eliminate all of the issues surrounding how the numbers were arrived at, because well-done budget narratives explain the numbers as well as the assumptions and the plans for the future.
10. It relates, in writing, financial results to strategies and to capital expenditures.

A well-done budget document should be able to (1) stand alone as an explanation of what's going on in any business, and (2) be used to measure the performance of that business, annually.

It should also extend throughout the operating plan period with sufficient explanation for any reader to see the linkage between the budget year and the out years. When strategies are properly overlaid with capital expenditures for several years, the resultant changes in the business mix should be explained easily, with the right narrative.

THE NARRATIVE TO SUPPORT THE NUMBERS

Many managers wonder why writing is such a necessary adjunct to planning. The major reason is that writing establishes a discipline and a commitment. In addition, it focuses managers' thinking on the following key points:

1. It forces them to stop and think again about how they have developed their planning assumptions and projections, and then, to explain it in writing.
2. It requires them, in writing, to do all the analysis necessary to be able to explain variances clearly. It makes managers think more about what should go into their planning assumptions in the first place, to reduce the potential for major variances. It also functions to fine tune their planning assumptions, because they have to explain variances from their planning assumptions as well as variances between their projections and what actually happened.
3. It allows for other managers to know about each other's area of responsibility, problems, and common planning assumptions.

Well-written plans are like good books; they tell the story of the business function by function. They clarify what everybody is doing, eliminate the unnecessary mystique about confidentiality, and detail where management wants the business to have passed by next year. They function as a chronological explanation of how management is planning to get from where they are to where they want to be. Well-written plans offer valuable insight to everyone involved in a common management endeavor. They really bring to the participating managers a more vivid sense of their interacting responsibilities.

7
How to Use the Budget to Manage and Control

The whole purpose of budgeting and developing the operating plan is to facilitate managing long-term growth while controlling short-term operations better. The management information system is the vehicle that produces the comparative data on the budget versus the actual, as well as key performance indicators for management on trends, and supplemental exception reports.

MARRIAGE OF THE BUDGET
AND THE ACCOUNTING SYSTEM

The budget data has to be broken down into monthly segments by using historical seasonalization patterns and taking into consideration known events, like, when products will be introduced, and people hired. It is often a good idea, when beginning the planning period, to build the budget data by month, where possible, in anticipation of this requirement.

To avoid being one of the many horror stories in business periodicals, it is important to have the same basic report formats and data base information for both the budget and the accounting system. In most cases, with minor adjustments, the accounting system can accommodate the budget format. So the budget is spread by month, and is input into the system, line item by line item. As business commences for the new year, the accounting system captures the actual data and compares it to the budget data, and calculates variances where they occur.

MONTHLY MANAGEMENT MEETING AND REPORT FORMATS

Monthly Performance Reports

Well-managed companies review results on a monthly basis, as soon as possible after the end of business for that month. Good financial accounting systems produce actual results that are accurate, timely, and in a format compatible with the planning process and format. Most accounting systems produce results in the profit and loss format for the current month (period), and compare those to the budget for the current month, as well as to the budget for that same month last year. They also accumulate data and produce year-to-date results. An example of such a report would be:

XYZ COMPANY

Profit & Loss Statement for the Month of _____

Current Period					$ (Thousands)	Year-to-Date				
Last Year	This Year	Bud-get	% Last Year	% Bud-get		Last Year	This Year	Bud-get	% Last Year	% Bud-get
					Sales					
					Cost of Sales					
					Gross Profit					
					Expenses					
					Profit/ (Loss)					

This format allows management to see rapidly how the business is performing on a monthly and year-to-date basis. By observing the percentages against both last year and the budget, you can ascertain readily all the information you need by category of profit and loss statement information. However, to achieve a more effective presentation of operating results, some narrative and selective data must be put into a format that is more digestible by management.

Monthly Management Report

Good monthly management reports facilitate the process of management, and save time by highlighting those things in any operating unit that require attention and decision making. The assembly of such a document requires the following format:

1. Narrative
2. Key Performance Indicators
3. Charts and Graphs
4. Financial Statements

The narrative should be a clear, brief explanation of business conditions and results of the month. An example of the narrative is:

Division Result XYZ COMPANY

Division Results for the Month of _____

Sales for ___(month)___ were $_____, which is X% of budget and X% of last year's sales for this month. Profits for the month were $_____ , X% of budget and X% ahead of this time last year. During the month the following happened: _____, _____ , and _____. We plan to watch these trends closely, and will report on them in the next report. This brings year-to-date results to sales of $_____ and profits of $_____, which are X% and X% of budget, and X% and X% of last year, respectively.

Of course, events of significance would be elaborated on, or a special report would be prepared, and appended to the monthly report. The purpose of the narrative is to present a succinct explanation of what happened last month as an introduction to the rest of the report.

The next part of the report should be key performance indicators. Key performance indicators are those major volume-related statistics about business operations that either make the business happen, or not happen. These trend indicators are also important to track for contingency planning purposes.

Key performance indicators are the most important statistics in the business, and should be ranked in order of their importance to making the business plan happen. When you are selling a product or service, as every business is, then some measure of sales (units, sales representatives' performance) is the most important key performance indicator. Sales would then be followed by the next most important indicator, let's say, collections of receivables from those sales made in previous accounting periods (days-of-sales outstanding). Then let's assume that inventory turnover is the next most important indicator (months-on-hand). A typical key performance indicator report would look like this:

XYZ COMPANY

Division Results for the Month of _____

Key Performance Indicators

	Last Half-Year						This Year										
	J	A	S	O	N	D	J	F	M	A	J	J	A	S	O	N	D
Sales Units																	
Days-of-Sales Outstanding																	
Months-on-Hand																	
Sales Rep's Returns																	
Mean Time Between Product Failures																	
Average Absenteeism																	

As you can see, this kind of report has actual data only, but it is the most significant data in terms of trends in the business. It is also important to note that the data has to reflect last year's results so that trends are apparent. This kind of report can be one of the most meaningful for both corporate and operating line management. To be most useful, a substantial amount of analysis has to be done in conjunction with the planning process to make sure that you are tracking the most important trend indicators of the future impact of current trends.

The next part of the report should be several charts and graphs on those key performance indicators about which management should be most concerned. Some typical examples are:

XYZ COMPANY

Division Results for the Month of _____

Sales Units

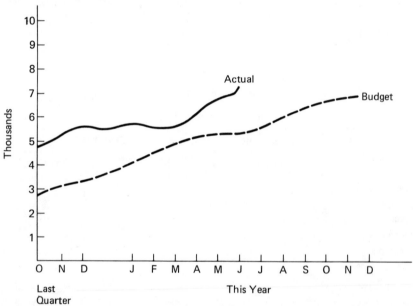

NOTE: When and where appropriate, these trend indicators should be monitored for proximity to trigger points at which contingency plans should be reviewed for implementation.

XYZ COMPANY

Division Results for the Month of _____

Sales Representation

	J	F	M	A	M	J	J	A	S	O	N	D
Northeast: Actual												
Budget												
Southeast: Actual												
Budget												
Midwest: Actual												
Budget												
Northwest: Actual												
Budget												
Southwest: Actual												
Budget												
National: Actual												
Budget												
Tenure: Actual												
Budget												

As these examples illustrate, one picture is worth a thousand words, in business as well as in other aspects of life. In reality, this form of presentation is very effective for displaying most key business results.

To review briefly, the narrative has been presented (summarizing the monthly results), then the key performance indicators, and then the charts and graphs. At this point in reviewing the monthly results, the majority of the explanation of evants is accomplished, so that by the time you get to the financial statements, those results are self-evident. This mode of presentation also allows for a clear dialogue among the management groups, unencumbered by any confusion related to financial terminology, as often happens when starting out to review operations by reviewing the financial statements first.

The result of the monthly management meeting is a continuing dialogue between the general manager and the respective functional managers, which may produce some action items (the need to do some additional analysis) for discussion at the next monthly management meeting. The next meeting should start with a review of the action items from the last meeting. The monthly review meeting functions as the control vehicle for corporate management over all the operating units, and the format of the reports for all of the units should be the same, in order to achieve the same efficiency as was accomplished in the annual business planning process.

The monthly management review meetings take place for the first three months (quarter) of the budget year. At the end of the first quarter there should be a quarterly review.

THE QUARTERLY REVIEW

The quarterly review is a mini-budgeting activity. It begins by comparing actual results for the first quarter to the business plan (the budget) for the quarter, as well as to the first quarter of last year. Then, the impact of the first quarter actual performance is evaluated in light of the business planning assumptions for the balance of the year. In most cases, there is a sufficient variance to warrant some kind of a reprojection of the balance of the year. Most reprojections have to do with changes in product mix and operating expenses. These reprojections do not usually require as major an effort as that which goes into building the annual plan, unless the variance from the budget in the first quarter is very significant. Once the exercise is completed, there is another meeting with corporate management wherein the quarterly review of operations takes place.

The format of the presentation is basically that of the profit and loss statement, in the following format:

XYZ COMPANY

A Division Quarterly Performance Review

| First Quarter | | | | | | Balance of the Year | | | | |
Last Year	This Year	Bud-get	% Last Year	% This Year		Last Year	Bud-get	Projec-tion	% Last Year	% Bud-get
					Sales					
					Cost					
					Gross Profit					
					Expenses					
					Profit/(Loss)					

In addition, other key financial ratios pertinent to the business are also discussed and presented in the quarterly review package. One of the most important aspects of the quarterly review, besides operating performance, is a review of capital expenditures and the discussion of strategic milestones. The quarterly review meeting really represents the forum for a performance review of the progress against the annual business plan (the budget), as well as a review of performance against the strategic milestones in the operating plan, and the capital expenditures related thereto. The format of the quarterly review presentation is:

1. A narrative explaining the first quarter results and discussing the projection that was made for the balance of the year as a result of actual business experience in the first three months; then any other required financial schedules.
2. A presentation of capital expenditures related to progress against operating plan strategies.

If a business unit is not performing well as compared to its strategic objectives, this quarterly review session can be the vehicle for curtailing further expenditures until performance improves, or for modifying the strategies. Likewise, if business is good, it can be an opportunity to obtain the approval to accelerate those successful strategies. Quarterly reviews allow corporate management to sort out all of the ongoing strategies, and constantly allocate and reallocate resources based upon the performance, or lack of performance, of each unit in the total corporate operation. They are another step in the constant activity required to have a well-controlled and -managed company.

After the quarterly review, the monthly management reporting begins again for the next three months (April, May, June) with a comparison now either to the budget, or to the projection for the balance of the year from the quarterly review. Performance is measured against the plan *or* the projection, month by month this way until the end of the first half (six months) of the year.

At the end of this period, or, six months into the budget year, there is another major review of operations (like the first quarter review) called the first-half review.

THE FIRST-HALF REVIEW

The first-half review is very similar in process to the first-quarter review. The first six months of actual results are compared to the first half of last year, and to the first six months of the budget. The variance from budget produced by the actual results represents the basis for reprojecting the balance of the year at this time (midyear), and schedules similar to those prepared for the first quarter are prepared for the six months of actual, last year, and the six months projected for the balance of the year. A narrative is prepared, likewise similar to the first-quarter narrative, detailing capital expenditures by strategy, as well as matching progress reports against strategic milestones.

There is then another major management meeting, to review results and make decisions on either continuing, accelerating, or delaying strategies, depending upon performance against strategic milestones of the respective operating units. Thus, we have the second of two annual major management and planning review meetings to measure performance against strategies. The monthly management meetings, in combination with the quarterly and first-half reviews, allow corporate management to keep very closely abreast of what's going on in each operating unit so that they can monitor constantly the strategic trends and accomplishments in the entire corporation.

After the first-half review, the monthly management reports become the control mechanism for the next three months (July, August, September), which lead into the annual planning cycle.

ANNUAL PLANNING CYCLE

There isn't usually a nine-month review because we are then back in the annual planning cycle which requires projecting year-end anyway. To review:

Controlling the Business Plan and Planning Cycle

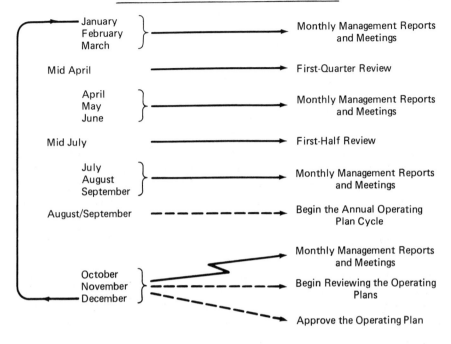

As you can see, one operating plan dovetails with the next, and as the business moves through the budget year, reprojecting expected annual results on a quarterly basis for the first half, the stage is being set for the planning assumptions for the next year's operating plan. The management information system plays an integral part in this process, collecting actual experience and comparing those results against the plan, as well as producing key performance indicators.

These days there is a proliferation of software packages available that can be run on small business computers to automate this entire process. In addition, some of the larger software marketers have modified their mainframe packages now to run at the micro level. This means that the sophistication and discipline of computerized planning, with all of the attributes associated with electronic spreadsheets and their what-if capabilities, are available to the small business.

Some of the more popular of these planning packages, like: Visicalc, Multiplan, Supercalc, Microplan, Financial Planner, Perfect Calc, and all of their competitors, are virtually alike in their ability to solve planning problems and manipulate management information. Future generations of software packages will become more English language-oriented in their operating instructions.

The more advanced of the current packages offer users the ability to create spreadsheets for budgets, forecasts, and cash flow analysis, and the capacity to evaluate the potential financial impact of any variety of what-if situations. Some of the existing software allows users to create models for financial planning and control, using English-like commands rather than anything that looks like a formula. These packages offer editing and report writing capabilities, as well.

To illustrate the interaction and interrelationship of operating plans:

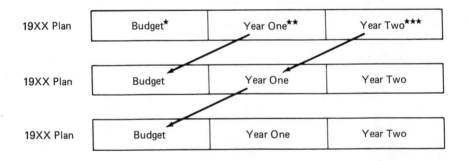

Notes: *Strategies are put in motion to move the business into position to continue that direction into Year One, assuming favorable performance.

**Strategies are submitted as part of the operating plan to get approval-in-principle to be included for capital expenditures in the next operating plan.

***Strategies are conceived under the assumption that the budget for Year One will be accomplished, and the plan for Year Two will be approved in principle.

This recycling and revaluation of strategies, and the constant comparison of plans to actual performance, represents the essence of good planning. A continuous focus on and review of the potential of alternative action plans for the future creates the discipline of systematized management. Going through this process of periodic measurement and analysis of key performance indicators and strategies has to make for better planners, and in turn, better managers.

8
How Long Does It Take for the System to Work?

The first planning exercise was like putting on a new pair of shoes and trying to walk in them. It was getting the management team together in a new way and forcing them through an exercise with which they probably felt uncomfortable.

INITIAL PLAN USUALLY NOT VERY GOOD

Consequently, while a good effort is usually made, the initial plan generally tends to be the historical number crunching exercise overlaid with some new words and new ideas. There is a natural tendency on the part of operating managers to revert quickly to their old operating styles after the first planning exercise.

It takes an unusually strong CEO to maintain the right kind of discipline throughout the exercise, because, in most cases, they, too are relatively new at the process. The *key* to success is maintaining the planning discipline by having good monthly management meetings, where trends and patterns are highlighted by reviewing performance indicators with a critical analysis and comparison to the planning assumptions. Key performance indicators are the most important items to review because they are the statistics that should be extrapolated to indicate how what's happening now will impact the company's ability to achieve their short-term (budgeted) goals and impact the overall strategies. It's very important to look beyond the traditional budget-to-actual and actual-to-last-year's financial results, if you really want to maintain that balance of the present (this year's goals) with the future (the strategic plan).

The next key ingredients are the quarterly and first-half reviews, because that is where the initial strategic milestones are measured. It is there that the planning assumptions are really tested, and hard decisions have to be made on the level of commitment to the initial plan.

It also becomes apparent during the first months of measuring actual performance against the "new" planning concept, whether or not "enough" thought went into developing the planning assumptions and details during the planning process. Were all the possibilities really well thought-out? Was there something we overlooked that we could have anticipated? It isn't easy to get out of the old fire-fighting mode and into the planning mode, where management doesn't *react* to problems, but tries to *anticipate* them.

In any case, the initial planning exercise tends to be stimulating, and does introduce the overall concept. Managers do respond, and develop an appreciation for thinking more futuristically about the business. One of the biggest benefits is that they develop a better understanding of their peers' problems, and they try to be more cooperative.

One effective technique is the continued use of an independent planning organization, or consultant, in the quarterly review process. Their objective input can keep clear the emphasis needed for the long-term strategic direction, from the natural tendency to return to the "business as usual" fire fight. Without this independent objective type of referee, there is almost always some level of confusion, because no one has done it before.

The biggest problem continues to be managers giving daily operational problems priority over the longer term plans just recently agreed to in the planning process. This tendency comes about because everyone wants to go back to doing what they like, know best, and feel comfortable with. For most managers new to planning, this is the most difficult task for them to handle. The other thing that happens is that managers forget their strategic priorities and try to work on everything at once. This causes tremendous confusion among their subordinates, and usually results in nothing getting done well. It's like having breakfast, lunch, and dinner served all at once.

SECOND PLAN MORE FRUSTRATING THAN THE FIRST

When it's time to begin next year's planning cycle, it is already fairly evident how successful the first effort was, because at least three quarters of the results are in on the first year (the budget). In addition, progress (or lack thereof) against the first set of strategies is also fairly obvious. With this information in hand, and a feeling for the kind of discipline that is required, for most managers, the second planning exercise is generally even more frustrating than the first.

Their attitude at the beginning of the second planning cycle is usually "here we go again staring into our crystal ball," but they are also concerned about trying to improve on what they thought was good the first time around. The problem tends to lie in the areas of creativity and intuitive thinking. Considering that most managers come up through the operating ranks, where most of their time was spent on weekly and monthly goal setting, it is easy to understand why they have some initial difficulty in thinking about objectives that are a year or two away.

They have attempted to do this the first time around, and in most cases, were only marginally successful. To ask them to improve on that performance tends to be quite frustrating.

It's common to find this situation after the first planning period:

1. The overall business has remained just about the same.
2. Some progress was made on a few strategies.
3. No real progress was made on the rest, but there was an awful lot of conversation about them.
4. The management team is frustrated by their lack of progress, but have talked to each other much more than ever before about the real problems of the business.
5. Everyone knows they have to spend more time trying to make the plan happen and less time doing what they like to do.

But the groundwork is there. It will improve with the next planning period — assuming management commitment is evident, managers want to contribute, and they see value in the team effort.

The second planning exercise, in terms of procedure, is simpler than the first, because strengths, weaknesses, and strategies don't have to be redone as thoroughly as when starting out. However, it is interesting to go back over the initial plans that were developed to make the strengths "more and better," and, improving upon weaknesses, to see what has really changed during the year, or what has happened because we wanted it to. The changes form the basis for reconsidering and reevaluating strategies.

Progress against strategies over the last year is probably the best learning experience in terms of measuring how realistic they were in the first place, and how the management team was able to deal with them. Discussing and rethinking performance against those strategies, in addition to studying how market conditions have changed over the year, should allow for better strategies to come out of the second planning exercise.

Another way to develop better plans the second time around is to rethink strategies in terms of their role in the portfolio of strategies, and to assess how management plans to allocate time and resources to strategies in the second planning cycle. Figure 8.1 can be helpful in this exercise. The first column requires management to list products, by-products, product concepts, or R & D projects in order of their sales and profit potential, or their best estimate of it. The next two columns just require a check (✓) to indicate when they became a strategy. The next three columns are for actual sales for last year (if there were any), sales for this year (if there will be any), and sales for next year (hopefully there will be some), respectively. The last column is used to designate the strategic priority of the strategy, and should be management's best estimate as to how they plan to use their time and the company's resources.

When completed, this form should be a clear indication of the consistency and clarity of planning thought that has gone into the planning process thus far. If the strategy that has the number one strategic priority was a strategy last year, but had no sales last year, no sales this year, and promises only marginal sales next year, I would wonder why management plans to allocate so much time on a strategy that obviously has a long lead time to generate any sales. While this may be an exaggerated example, when all the information is completed on all the strategies, it can be quite revealing, and cause for a better allocation of time and resources on the potentially more

PORTFOLIO ANALYSIS WORKSHEET
(This form has been designed to simplify the process of
completing the traditional portfolio analysis matrix.)

		Became a Strategy ✓		Sales			Strategic Priority*
		This Yr.	Last Yr.	Last Yr.	This Yr.	Next Yr.	
HIGHEST ↑	Redesign Widget			$420,000	$375,000	$525,000	1
	Grass Collection			$350,000	$295,000	$325,000	2
	End Marketing Widgets			$ 60,000	$ 42,000	$ 31,000	4
GROWTH POTENTIAL							
	Improve Company Image			—	—	—	7
LOWEST ↓							
	Redesign Company Logo			—	—	—	10

Products,   By-products,   Product Concepts, R & D Projects

*Should determine how you allocate management time and resources.

Fig. 8.1. Portfolio analysis worksheet.

meaningful strategies. There should be a fairly good correlation between growth potential, sales, and strategic priority.

The second planning exercise is basically the same in terms of forecasting results for the operating plan period, once the revised strategies have been agreed upon. The same kind of planning document is prepared, but this time, probably with more realism.

Performance tracking is basically the same too, but the attention to accomplishing strategic objectives usually becomes more serious, because it's the second time around, and now management performance is also considered. It now becomes more and more obvious how well each manager can plan and how dependent they really are on each other to make their respective strategies happen.

There is still that problem of self-discipline that managers have to develop to concentrate on their strategies and not revert back to the day-to-day fire fighting. It's still a good idea to have the professional planning organization or consultant participate in the development of the second plan, for efficiency, and as a confidence builder for the respective managers. Likewise, it's good to invite professional criticism at the quarterly review sessions for the second year's operating plan. At the end of the second full cycle (annual planning exercise and quarterly reviews) you can usually conclude the involvement of outside professionals as participants in the planning process, with the understanding that they may be called upon for guidance if the process gets "fuzzy" again.

THIRD PLANNING EXERCISE SHOWS REAL RESULTS

With two years under their belts, most managers have a much better appreciation of strategic planning management. They understand it better conceptually, and they have witnessed personally what they didn't know about what they thought they knew. More importantly, they have experienced a more in-depth understanding of the totality of the business and the functional interrelationships. They now appreciate the team concept and how they must help each other, and the CEO, to achieve their common goals.

All of this experience over two years produces embarrassing and enlightening moments that bring the management team together and slowly start to form a bond. Another thing happens; everyone starts to talk the same language — planning. Everyone starts to think futuristically, and to put away permanently the concern with the past and present.

The third planning exercise is usually anticipated and much more cooperative than the first two. Everybody feels more confident and comfortable with what they are doing. Strategies are refined; the writing is better, and mostly standardized; and planning slowly starts to be "preached" through the ranks.

The results of the third cycle are usually much closer to the plan, and plans begin to be modified much sooner than in the first two exercises. Contingency plans are actually used, and decisions made much more objectively and calmly than in the "past." The quarterly review sessions become more professional, and the entire process of management becomes more orderly. Everyone forgets to wonder why it wasn't like this before.

EACH FOLLOWING CYCLE IS EASIER
AND THE RESULTS BETTER

After the third cycle, the planning routine becomes standard operating procedure. Operational reviews are easier, and results usually better. Planning becomes the integral part of management that it should be, which is reflected in more efficient operations.

After a while, depending on the growth of the organization, a planning department may be established to relieve the last burden on the operating managers; then, the planning process becomes routine and fine tuned.

In conclusion, actual experience is always the best measure of progress, and the following represents the actual thoughts of the CEO of a small company on his experience in implementing strategic planning:

HOW XYZ INDUSTRIES BEGAN
THE STRATEGIC PLANNING PROCESS

Q. Why Strategic Planning?

A. "Motivation from a Director of the Company who was more interested in long range versus short range; not so much attention on what happened in the past quarter and what will happen the next quarter, but where are we going in the long range and how are we going to get there?"

Q.   Did you plan before?

A.   "Yes! We did, but the emphasis was totally financial, that is, what we expected to do quantitatively in sales and earnings rather than *how* we planned to do it. However, the reverse is true with Strategic Planning, because we now:

1. Set general objectives.
2. Determine *how* we are going to achieve these objectives step by step.
3. And, in achieving these objectives, what it will mean in terms of dollars of sales, what it will cost, and how much we will make as a result of doing it each step along the way."

Q.   How did you get started (without going into too much detail)?

A.   "1.   Set a mission for ourselves.
2.   Reviewed the strengths and weaknesses of the company, objectively and realistically. We knew what they were, but we never set them down in so vivid a fashion.
3.   Reviewed opportunities and problems.
4.   Developed some general strategies."

Q.   What results did you get from the first plan?

A.   "Just in formulating the general strategies, we ended up with a much better idea as to how (and specifically who), we're going to achieve some of the objectives that we've had for some time. Better financial planning, cash flows, budgets, profits, etc. We also made a major change in thinking, which resulted in a critical analysis of how the Company was progressing. We went from emphasis on P & L, by division, to P & L by product, and we are now able to focus, in more of a portfolio fashion on how best to use our resources, while at the same time evaluating product lines. We learned the importance of developing contingency plans. This became more apparent as the initial plan was implemented, simply because some of our plans came to a screeching halt for one reason or another, but mostly because we tried to do too much all at once. We found that contingency planning is extremely difficult because it causes us to *think* in terms of the possible failure of a plan. It's hard to accept the fact that you can fail as a manager."

Q. What did you learn during the implementation of this plan?

A. "There are two important problem areas that have to be addressed:

1. Who should be responsible for strategies — very important.

   a. Regarding responsibility, only one person should be assigned to *oversee* each strategy.

   b. Numerous people can be responsible for achieving certain aspects of the strategy with all of them reporting to the one individual who is responsible for that particular strategy.

   c. Example: Development and introduction of a new product line. One person can be assigned to the field testing; one person can be assigned to the writing up of the tests that should be used at the field test; one person may actually be responsible as a liaison between the testing and the corporation; one person can be responsible for the introduction and publicity of the new product; one for the sales training; etc. The important thing is that *only one person is responsible for the total strategy*, and all of these other individuals basically report to him. This often may go across corporation/organizational lines, that is, you can have one Vice President reporting to another Vice President in terms of a particular strategy in a true project management sense.

2. The actual written outline, that is, mechanical layout of the strategy, has to be clear so it can be assigned and controlled properly.

   a. The "assignment" form that we developed incorporates:

      • A descriptive title of the strategy. Example: Introduction of a new product line.
      • A listing of strategy steps.

- A date by which each step is to be completed (quarterly).
- The individual responsible for the total strategy.
- The respective managers responsible for individual parts of the total strategy.
- The estimated costs to accomplish the strategy, step by step, if possible.
- The expected return.
- Related capital expenditures.
- Contingency plans, or what do we do if it doesn't work.

b. Forms should be easy-to-use operational tools for follow-up and guidance.

c. You have to have a strict follow-up to determine if the strategies are being accomplished. How? Starts with the CEO – he *is* responsible for the whole plan. CEO goes to the manager responsible for each strategy on a periodic basis throughout the year. In our case, it was at least every couple of months, with a formal status report or discussion due on a quarterly basis. I deal with only *one* individual per strategy. All of the strategies were kept in a binder for easy reference – one that by the end of the year should look very dog-eared. The strategies must have teeth, particularly as they relate to the reporting function. By teeth I mean such things as written or verbal reports on specified dates not only to show *how* this strategy is developing but to indicate *what* is specifically being done to develop the strategy. Example: New Product. Questionnaire to be developed for field testing. Results of field testing by companies: Marketing plans developed by sales manager.

d. Pitfalls that I observed:

   1. Other than lack of teeth in the plan, one pitfall is trying to accomplish too much.
   2. Don't go into too much detail on plans; allow flexibility.

e. One other item that we learned from implementing this plan was that it makes the *financial planning considerably easier* when we have some idea of where we're going."

Q. The Second Plan — What happened?

A. "It was much easier than the first, because we had a track to run on and all we did was revise some of the basic analysis of the company. It's not necessary to rewrite the plan totally but rather to spend time to review and revise what we did the first time. At the same time review where we are on our current strategies and start thinking about ways to improve them in the coming months. We added new strategies where necessary and eliminated others, or upgraded those that were still viable. It was easier to complete the second plan, and particularly if some of the early strategies have been somewhat successful, because it proves to the managers involved the value of taking the time for strategic planning."

Q. What has this new concept of strategic planning done for your company?

A. "It put more emphasis on methods of achieving objectives rather than on just what those objectives should be. It helped management and the total company work more as a team, since we had a rail to run on. It gave us a definite advantage, I believe, over those firms that did not do this type of planning, because we had more clarity of purpose. It made for improved communications between the different levels of the organization because we all had a better understanding of what we were doing as a whole. It gave us a much needed and better means of evaluating our progress or lack of progress, specifically by understanding better the role that each product and strategic concept played in the future of our company. It just simply helped us manage better."

9
Major Advantages of
Good Planning and Budgeting

As has been stressed throughout this book, planning is an integral part of management. Good managers are constantly planning: planning for the present as well as the future. Written plans create a commitment, and function as the best way to communicate to everyone else in any organization who has a need to know what the plan is, how we are going to make it happen, and who will be responsible. It's plain good employee relations, too.

ESTABLISHES A DISCIPLINE

Good formalized planning establishes the planning discipline. Planning becomes standard operating procedure, and with it comes improved controls, and better management information and performance tracking. The longer any organization has adopted formalized planning, the farther down in the organization the discipline has gone.

At the beginning of the process it is looked upon as another unpleasant chore, but as its value becomes more and more appreciated, planning becomes more of a natural part of the operating environment. When everyone knows what the plan is, they have more comfortable parameters within which to work. When there is no plan, everyone has a vague sense of direction, which by its very nature fosters inefficiency. Perhaps even more important than a clear sense of direction, are the contingency plans that have been well thought-through to deal with results substantially over, or under, plan actual experience. So rather than the helter-skelter frequent crises of the past, there is an organized way of dealing with faster-than-expected growth or decline in business conditions.

With a plan you can manage the plan; *without* a plan you are managed by the business.

The other major aspect of planning is the better utilization of resources throughout the organization. Rather than everyone generally running around in an uncoordinated way, planning concentrates the resources of the organization on specific strategies. Those strategies are closely tracked, and when it becomes apparent that one is about to bear fruit and needs additional funding, the others that haven't reached that stage yet can be put on the back burner, or aborted.

GETS STAFF TO WORK AS A TEAM
TOWARDS COMMON GOALS AND OBJECTIVES

While conceptually everyone is supposed to be working together cooperatively, in unplanned environments people tend to work against each other more often than not. There is a tendency for the people in each functional area to set up their own small kingdom and to work diligently to blame *other* functional areas for not cooperating (which has resulted in *their* not being able to perform somehow). In these situations, good communication is almost nonexistent, and inefficiency and duplication permeate the entire operation. Without a shared understanding, the senior players will naturally veer off in different directions.

With a good planning system, everyone has to cooperate because they become part of the total goals and objectives of the organization. The strategic planning process is designed in such a way that it fosters and requires a team effort. Understanding the plan in itself is a giant step towards eliminating the functional problems of the past. This, coupled with a clearer understanding of everyone else's problems, creates a more cooperative climate. However, if an organization is headed in the wrong direction, the last thing it needs is to get there more efficiently.

The monthly management meetings function as a forum to clarify operating problems in a group setting, with the CEO as the moderator. The constant emphasis on monthly performance against the plan in combination with quarterly and first-half reviews keeps the team functioning as a team. In addition, their respective subordinates are working towards the same goals, too.

By making management a joint effort of all functional areas, with clearly set goals (set by management), it is very hard to attribute poor results to anything but a breakdown in the team. To reinforce this with very specific strategic milestone assignments completely eliminates any opportunity to return to the finger pointing excuses of the past. It also becomes easier to make important decisions based solely on concrete, agreed upon, operational criteria (such as ROI considerations) fit to current sales and marketing plans, or fit to existing human resource capabilities.

Unless senior management consciously sets strategy as a team, you risk having the organization's direction developed implicitly, or by others inside or outside the organization: middle management, the government, banks, competition, or labor unions.

Perhaps the easiest way to illustrate the importance of the team concept and the need for having common strategic goals and objectives is to put the following questions to any CEO and management team.

1. What is the mission of your organization? Where do you want to be in the next five years?
2. What has happened lately because you planned it to happen?
3. Do you know the details of your organization's strategy? Would each of the other key managers share your feelings about the future strategic direction of the organization?
4. Are your strategies sufficiently clear so that you and the other key managers around you can readily agree on what new products and markets your current strategy would include and exclude?
5. Is your future strategy clearly determining what you plan, project, and budget, or are your plans, projections, and budgets determining your strategy?
6. Is your future strategy clearly determining your decisions relating to acquisitions, capital expenditures, and new products, or are such decisions determining your strategy?

7. Is the overall performance of your organization and its products reviewed on both strategic accomplishments and operating results?

The more of these questions that can be answered "yes," the closer you are to having a team capable of putting in motion an integrated set of action plans aimed at improving market position.

CREATES A SYSTEM FOR MANAGING

Strategic planning is a management system. It is a process that clarifies decision making by focusing analysis on the three key ingredients that are necessary for the ultimate success of any business:

Products

What are the major attributes of each of our products?
What's wrong with them?
Why are our products better than our competitors' products?
Who buys our products, and why do they buy them?
What by-products can we create from our existing products?
What other products can we make with our existing resources?
What pricing flexibility do we have?
How can we reduce costs by product?
What technology do we need to invest in to maintain the leading edge?

Markets

What are the key performance indicators of the future for the markets we are in?
Can we expand the markets for our products through:

1. New geographical areas?
2. New packaging?
3. New advertising and promotion?
4. New sizes/shapes?
5. Creative pricing, dealing?
6. New by-products?
7. New sales techniques?
8. Better training of our sales force?

What trends do we see in our markets? Favorable/Unfavorable?
What are we doing about those trends?
Do we know the profile of our perfect customer?
What does the economy do to our markets?
What technology is developing?

Competitors

Do we know who *all* of them are?
What are our strengths and weaknesses compared to theirs?
What does it appear that their strategies are?
How do we plan to react to their strategies?
What customers do they have that we would like to have?
What plans do we have to get those customers?
What is the one thing that each competitor seems to do better than us?
What is our strategy to deal with those competitive disadvantages?
How are we planning to prevent competitors from incorporating our strengths?
What is the impact of foreign competition?
What are we doing about it?

If you can answer these questions and put together a good portfolio analysis of your products, what you have to do will become so obvious that you will wonder what you were doing up to now. Creative strategy making is pulling away the layers of comfort associated with the "business as usual" complacency that sets into every business, over time, and results in management:

1. Losing competitive focus.
2. Failing to think creatively about options.
3. Limiting themselves to direct old-fashioned head-on competition.

The process of continuous evaluation of products, markets, and competition allows you to evaluate the best of theirs, and to incorporate the best of theirs and yours with your planning for the future. After all, business is anticipating the future and planning for it, rather than reacting to it when it's too late.

RESULTS IN OBJECTIVITY

One of the biggest problems with managing in an unplanned environment is that when you are constantly fire fighting and practicing the worst kind of management, crisis management, you lose objectivity completely. You can't think clearly when you are a fireman because you are constantly running around putting out fires. One day your fire extinguisher may run out of chemicals, and then you're really out of business.

Strategic planning lets you step back from the daily routine and regain your objectivity, but you must take the time to do it. You have to invest time to save time. Once you can see more clearly again you can start to really manage again, rather than be managed.

It isn't easy for everyone to get started, because most top executives, especially in smaller firms, have gotten where they are because they have been successful operationally — dealing with the day-to-day details of the business. This is where they feel most comfortable. However, once you can breathe some fresh air into them by getting them away from the business to start to learn about strategy making, it oftentimes becomes a revelation. It's a pleasant surprise to know that there really is a way to "create" the future, or at least that there are several alternatives to what we're doing now.

With a plan you can think objectively, because you have the comfort that today's business is being tracked and managed. You have built up that confidence by putting in place a working operating plan that produces good management information every month, and keeps you focused on the impact of today's business on the plans you've made for the future. You can now decide objectively what to do in terms of exercising a contingency plan, or modifying some of your future planning assumptions rather than leaping into the lurch with your fire extinguisher.

Good planning and budgeting does establish a much needed discipline and systematic ordering of managing. It does bring the management team together to work towards common goals. It does create a system for managing all of the people, the plant, and financial resources, objectively.

10
Common Pitfalls of Beginning
the Planning Process

As has been stated throughout, planning is not easy. It's hard, con-centrative work. It requires creative and intuitive thinking by a wide range of managers experienced at operating management, but generally inexperienced at planning management.

It requires people to change their way of thinking and working from short-term to long-term. They have to learn how to speak a new language — planning. They have to work together as a team. Their performance against their plan is reflected in their paychecks.

LACK OF TOTAL COMMITMENT BY THE CEO

In all of the books and articles written, and the surveys that have been taken over the years, the major reason for ineffective planning that comes up time and time again is the lack of commitment by the CEO and senior management. This issue of commitment is compli-cated due to the myriad of confusing management styles.

Most evident among these confusing styles is the CEO who con-stantly gives lip service to how good the planning process is at his company, but never participates in any planning meetings, and con-tinuously gives directions contrary to the published plans.

His equally guilty brother participates in strategy meetings, but allows the management team to develop a proliferation of strategies beyond anyone's ability ever to achieve. This results in such a dilu-tion of effort that, usually, none of the strategies are ever really totally implemented, and a new equally numerous set of strategies emerges from the next planning session.

The third kind of misguided CEO does it by the numbers. His team most likely has step-by-step guidelines, their own set of forms, and probably some computer "models" to help in the process. This group turns out a very professional looking plan that appears to be supported by an abundance of scientifically developed rationale in a beautifully bound package. Unfortunately, these statistically oriented plans oftentimes bear no resemblance to the real world, and prove to be very difficult to reconcile with actual operating results.

Over time, management becomes disenchanted with the process; managers contribute only to the extent that they feel satisfies their political commitment, and continue to manage as they see fit. Without a total commitment by management to a rational process of planning, it becomes discredited, and just another academic exercise.

Effective planning requires the dedicated participation of the management team throughout the entire process of development and implementation. This must also encompass review and revision sessions.

POOR INTRODUCTION OF THE CONCEPTS

Another reason why some organizations don't get off to a good start is because they lack objectivity. As has been discussed throughout, planning is a conceptual exercise that requires intuitive and creative thinking. Unfortunately, there are no manuals on how to become creative; creative thinking tends to be more the product of good basic "brainstorming," or really thinking about all of the business options objectively. Sometimes it's very hard to get the team thinking in any way other than how they have been thinking after working together for so long and having a sort of built-in overfamiliarity with each other.

Some CEOs decide to hire a professional planner to do the plan for them. This approach can take two forms:

1. Hire a professional planner to *do* the plan for a consulting fee.
2. Hire a professional planner as an employee to help the management team plan, and to guide them in the process.

The usual problem with the first approach is that if you hire a professional planner to put the plan together for you, then in most cases, it becomes his plan and not yours. While the management team experiences some sort of an education in the planning process in this approach, it tends to be more superficial than not. When it comes time again to go through the annual planning cycle again, the majority of managers usually feel unsure of how to do it without the direction of the professional planner.

The other approach of hiring a professional planner to join the company as an employee has a slightly better chance if the planner has especially good political skills, can learn the business quickly, and is given the proper authority within the right overall climate. The chance of all of these things happening is unlikely in most companies. One of several things happens to the professional planner who is hired as an employee to help the management team to plan. First, and most often, the planner is given a vague introduction by the CEO, and consequently, no one on the management team understands what the planner is supposed to do; initially, they don't accept the planner as a peer; and probably, they will not cooperate readily. Unless there is a clear directive as to the level of authority and responsibility of the planner, as well as direction on how the management team is to cooperate with the planner, he will become utterly frustrated and ineffective. The best way to introduce the new planning function is at a staff meeting where the entire process is explained, support materials distributed, and the planner given an opportunity to make a presentation.

The second thing that happens frequently is that the new planner is forced to report to someone other than the CEO, most often, the controller or vice president of Finance. If the company hasn't planned before, by doing this, you are putting the planner in the awkward position of having to educate his boss in the basics of planning, while trying to work with his boss's peers. Frequently, the peers will be heard asking the planner's boss, "Do you know what he's talking about?" This approach is a very difficult one, and also tends to subvert the planner's effectiveness. When new planning people are hired to formulate and implement planning in an unplanned environment, they really should report directly to the CEO and work with the management team with the understanding that they are engaged in a joint venture with the CEO.

The third thing that happens is that the planner has difficulty getting down to the fundamentals with the management team, or he intimidates them, or cannot demonstrate a good understanding of their business, and related problems. Most professional planners have been involved in sophisticated planning environments, and when they have to return to basics it is difficult and frustrating. Sometimes this professionalism can become intimidating to the uninitiated. It is also quite a task to try to implement planning and learn about the technical complexities of the business at the same time. In very technically oriented companies, managers tend to discredit quickly those who cannot quickly grasp the nuances of their world.

So the new planner has to be an especially adroit politician, a fast learner, and must possess the ability to talk about planning from the most basic concept to the most sophisticated technique. To solve this problem, the CEO should use a screening methodology or a search firm experienced in selecting planners for different planning environments.

INSUFFICIENT PARTICIPATION BY MANAGERS

In order to be effective, planning demands participation. The point has been made several times throughout the text that the process is more valuable than the plan. That means that the joint effort of the management team coming together frequently in the planning process to identify problems and to struggle to be creative together is an extremely enlightening experience for everybody. If some of the members don't participate fully, then you don't derive the full benefit. It's much like an athletic team or military group with some members not fully trained. When it comes time to perform they are not able to present the most synchronized effort.

The exercise will be most effective when participation is required by the CEO. However, accomplishing this requires the right kind of introduction to the concepts, and good guidance throughout the initial process. Initially, managers that are new to planning need a lot of direction.

Without getting all of the managers' best input, the quality of the plan suffers in direct proportion to their lack of concern. Insufficient participation undermines good planning, as does the superficial input from "quick and dirty" exercises.

Planning is an intuitive and conceptual thinking process. It isn't something that can be done on the spur of the moment, or in the midst of confusion. Good plans take days and weeks of analysis, review, and solid thinking with subordinates, managers, and staff. Only after they have been well thought-out and analyzed should they be submitted.

FAILURE TO MARRY COMPENSATION WITH PLANNING

Considering the effort and time that are put into planning, it's a shame that some companies don't have an effective mechanism for relating performance against the plan, to compensation. The incentive created by compensating managers for their ability to make their plans work contributes significantly to the dynamics of the process.

Far too many potentially good plans have floundered due to the lack of a good financial incentive to make them happen. The best way to achieve a good planning discipline is to pay for performance by rewarding those managers who can plan well, and financially chastising those who cannot.

Good managers look for challenging compensation plans that increase reward in direct proportion to their ability to achieve specific strategic milestones and related financial objectives. Poor managers are content to collect their pay without any real concern about the condition of the business. Even good managers lose their initiative when their performance isn't recognized with financial compensation.

Compensation planning is good management, and without an adequate plan you will lose good managers. It's another element in the overall scheme having to do with establishing good management policies and procedures.

INADEQUATE AND INCONSISTENT FOLLOW-UP

Plans are meant to be monitored periodically. Strategies are developed with very specific strategic milestones. Budgets, operating plans, and their related strategies have to be controlled if a strategic plan is to succeed. Infrequent and inconsistent monitoring significantly dilutes the process.

Likewise, inadequate reviews tend to discredit the level of detail and effort that went into developing the strategy in the first place. If managers don't feel that their plans are being monitored, they won't be as diligent in their preparation of future plans. Another related circumstance that develops is the lack of follow-up on special analysis projects related to plan versus actual variances, capital expenditure projects, and/or market research.

Most managers make the general assumption that monthly, quarterly, and semiannual reviews are normal operating procedure. If these reviews do not take place then they adopt the attitude that "Management doesn't care, so why should I?" Understandably, this eventually leads to morale problems.

Well-managed companies have a systematic review process whereby plans are methodically reviewed against actual experience, and variances are thoroughly analyzed month by month. This is the only way that the future impact of current trends can be identified, and appropriate action taken either to stay on plan or to modify plans in an orderly fashion.

11
The Interrelationship of Planning with Corporate Culture in the Creation of Shared Values

CORPORATE CULTURE:
WHAT IT IS AND HOW IT COMES TO BE

Culture, by nature, is hard to get your arms around because it is caught up in the ebb and flow of living, and as such is embodied in the people that populate any organization. This makes a simple definition elusive other than to say that the culture of any organization is created by the interacting dynamics of the people that work there. This attempt at a definition has to be modified to include the fact that the corporate culture tends to be heavily weighted towards the influence that the leaders of any specific organization have on the culture of that organization due to the inherent structure that is necessary to make most organizations work. With this in mind, a modified explanation of corporate culture is that it represents the influence that the leaders, or senior managers, and especially the chief executive have on the organization, that tends to permeate the daily work environment and create a climate for the employees and an image for the enterprise. In other words, the attitudes, values, ethics, life styles, and to a great extent, the personalities of chief executives and their immediate subordinates create the culture of every organization. It naturally follows then that every organization has its own customized culture, or personality.

In some organizations this culture is easy to see and has created the image for which the company is known, internally and externally, a la IBM, AT&T, GE, and many others. The culture creates negative as well as positive images, which is clearly illustrated in the periodic surveys on the best and worst managed companies, as well as in a wide variety of articles in almost every edition of one magazine or periodical that makes up the business press. One of the many mysteries of corporate culture is that in many organizations, most of the people that work for these enterprises, and some of the senior executives, are unaware of what the culture is, and what kind of an image that culture has created in the world around them. In other organizations the culture is less clear, and generally, this "fuzzy" state of culture is the result of constantly changing management, or because a "safe state" of business as usual has been in effect for some time. Fuzzy cultures are usually apparent in firms that are in dull, mature industries run by caretaker-type managers, or in highly regulated industries where there is little opportunity or need to worry about competitive threats. Other examples of "fuzzy cultures" are firms whose senior management have gone to sleep with hefty compensation plans, or who are patiently waiting to retire, and obviously do not want to rock the boat. In these circumstances nothing happens because there is no incentive to make anything happen. Consequently, the rest of the employees are placed in a state of limbo, and the culture for them becomes "fuzzed up." All of this shouldn't come as a surprise, because all companies are run by people, and just because someone runs a company it doesn't change their basic hierarchy of needs, nor does it instill in them some magic feeling that forces them to be conspicuously conscious of the best interests of the employees, stockholders, customers, or the community.

Culture begins developing in an organization when the management team has had sufficient time working together to establish a politically comfortable or obviously uncomfortable relationship that most likely will not change. The only other situation where culture develops quickly is in those organizations totally dominated by the CEO, in which there is a simple culture — that of the CEO. When senior managers keep coming and going in any organization, the reasons are usually quite obvious, and the culture is not good. Getting back to those firms where most of the team stays in place for some time, the culture results from the interaction of the management team: how they manage the business; how that's perceived by the marketplace, the public at large, the stockholders, and the employees.

Usually, the longer the key players have been in place the easier it is to interpret the culture.

TYPICAL KINDS OF CULTURES

Since every company has its own culture it is impossible to do them all justice, but since all are run by people, some of the more obvious ones can be categorized and described. Before discussing these typical kinds of cultures it is important to recognize that in the world of managers there are those who are sophisticated (have studied and try to practice scientific management) and those who are unsophisticated (don't know anything about management but pretend that they do). To the latter group, corporate culture has something to do with history, the arts, or what nationality someone is. The culture in organizations that are run by this unsophisticated group generally tends to be quite confused because these managers usually operate in a state of emergency at all times. The word strategy to the unsophisticated manager is as foreign as Chinese or Arabic. In these organizations I guess you could say that the culture is truly that of the leader, and standard operating procedure is one more day just like yesterday. In this environment, while the senior unsophisticated managers may not really understand what culture means, the culture is quite clear.

My description of typical kinds of cultures is designed for employees and the marketplace to recognize.

The Excellent Culture

The excellent culture tends to be a way of planned corporate life where the organization has published its purpose in being (its mission) and works diligently to get that message to the lowest level within the organization. There is a constant emphasis on communication about the organization and how its plans are working. There is also a conscientious effort to involve as many managers as is practical in the planning process, and to make everyone who works for the company feel as if they are part of the team (corporate family). In these organizations planning is standard operating procedure, performance is related to the plans, and appraisals (plan and people) are usually held at quarterly, or at least semi-annual intervals. In other words, everybody in the organization knows what the plan is, what their role in the plan is, and how they are doing. The best example of this is that you can walk into these organizations and ask any manager "how's the plan?" and they will tell you about it for as long as you want to listen. You can walk into other organizations and ask "how's the plan?" and the answer will be "what plan?".

The Fuzzy Culture

As stated before, fuzzy cultures are usually apparent in organizations where one of the following circumstances prevails:

1.   Revolving door management.
2.   Dull, mature industry, managed by caretaker managers.
3.   Old management teams, about to retire, gone to sleep.
4.   Fat cat executives, hefty salaries, don't rock the boat, they are usually into other things.

Fuzzy cultures are easy to see from the outside, but not so easy to see for those on the inside. This is especially true for those who don't seem to understand what corporate culture is all about and how it affects them.

The Awful Culture

Awful cultures are generally characterized by crisis management, great and constant confusion, and fires that never seem to get put out. The climate in these organizations, for most of the employees, (except those totally oblivious to everything) is frustrating and unpleasant. Most of these organizations seem to be run by the owners (or their family), or by a lunatic who seems to be self-possessed by some intuitive feeling for what is the right thing for everybody to do every day.

It is important to realize that the size of the organization has nothing to do with which one of these kinds of cultures are present. They are evident in small, medium, and large organizations.

HOW CULTURES CHANGE

Since the culture of any organization is derived from the people in it, and especially from the leaders, there are only a few ways that any corporate culture can change: and both have to do with changing the people in some way. The first way is to replace some or all of the key players, or the chief executive, with others more sensitized to the importance of building an excellent culture. The second way is to try to change the way the key players think and act. Usually, the only way that can be done is to have the management team go through a strategic planning exercise to get them to sort out their strengths and weaknesses; figure out where they want to go and how they are going to try to get there; and then create the mission for the enterprise, the people in it, the owners, and the community.

It would be nice if it were so easy, but in reality it's quite difficult and sometimes impossible to change a culture if the senior managers aren't truly and totally committed. What that means is that there are many companies that have strategic plans on paper, but not in the minds of the management team. In those companies the planners wonder what they are doing there, get frustrated, and leave, because the plans are nothing but beautifully bound lip service to the strategic planning process.

PLANNING AND CULTURE

Planning goes on in many ways in most organizations, and even those who don't seem to have a plan have something that in their minds resembles a plan, even if it's only the annual budget. In most cases you could say that planning and culture are an integral part of the organization because the culture really drives the plan, or lack of a plan.

Informal Planning

Informal planning is most easily recognized in the form of the truly entrepreneurial CEO who has the plan in his head, and exercises his mental plan by the intuitive flashes that the employees find out about usually after the fact. It's also evident in the secretive meetings held infrequently by the key players, to plot "competitive strategy," which, likewise, never gets communicated to the rest of the team. Informal planning generally comes as a surprise to those who are supposed to implement these plans. Another classic example of informal planning is the annual budget, which is last year plus or minus something, and with no contingency plans for "What are we going to do if we don't make the budget?"

Informal planning done by solitary planners or groups of internal CIA operatives, where nothing ever gets written down, is a symptom of that kind of a culture. Its key ingredients are:

1. Does anybody know what the plan is?
2. Why are we doing this?
3. What happened to what's his name?
4. Fire! Fire! Fire!
5. What are we supposed to do today; he's not in.

Formal Planning

Formal planning, on the other hand, usually has evolved over a long period of time and manifests itself in the annual planning cycle, quarterly reviews, strategic milestones, special studies, acquisitions, divestitures, and the old standby, portfolio analysis. Formal planning is characterized by the strategic planning staff, sensitivity analysis, MBAs, contingency plans, operating plans, and "constant planning."

However, in most organizations that practice formal planning, there is an awareness and appreciation for the value of planning, and the language of planning has become part of the cultural communications system. If you don't use the right words there is obviously something wrong with you, or you must be new. These organizations have cultural structure, and the longer they have been at it the easier it is to see the culture. It's evident in their annual reports, their press releases, their public relations, and their overall corporate communications. Over time, this formalized planning system, especially for those organizations that have made it work well, like IBM, GE, et al, has become their cultural trademark. Their cultural planning system produces human products, e.g., an IBMer. Every IBMer looks the same, talks the same, and acts the same. It's corporate cultural programming — just like creating a "Moonie" or a "Hare Krishna."

Impact of Planning on Culture

The obvious product of an excellent culture speaks for the impact that planning can have on culture. Can all companies achieve an excellent culture? Probably not, because not all the people want an excellent culture, for what is, I hope, a variety of obvious reasons. Should all companies try to achieve an excellent culture? If it's within the power of those who recognize the value of having a good culture, it's certainly worth aspiring to, and at least the exercise will be enlightening.

We are finally entering a new era of management sensitivity to what was previously called social responsibility, ethics, and equal rights. We are also fully immersed in an international battle for survival. There really isn't any time anymore for members of the management team to compete with each other instead of with their competitors. Those organizations that will survive the future will do so based upon their ability to plan and to use all the tools available to them, including their most important resource — their people. Only recently, with the publication of a few books, has the obvious become a revelation.

One of my favorite expressions is "Companies don't plan to fail; they just fail to plan." People are the same way. Since all organizations are made up of people, and most people don't plan, then why should it come as such a great surprise that the organization has no plan? Everyone agrees that planning is a good thing, but only a few have a career plan. Why is it that people don't like to plan? Because it requires them to do three things that they don't like to do: to take the *time* (nobody every has any), to *think* (hard work), and to *write* (the author can be traced) their thoughts. Time, thinking, and writing are the essence of planning. It's necessary to take the time to think about: why we're doing what we're doing; what we really want to be doing; developing the strategies to get from where we are to where we want to be; and then writing all of that down so everybody involved with us knows what that is too. It's much easier than trying to catch those other people who are supposed to be on the team to ask them why they're doing what they're doing, only to find that they're too busy to tell you, and nothing is written down anywhere to help *you* either. In these cases, which, unfortunately seem to be in the majority, you are left to your own devices. No wonder we have "awful" cultures.

SHARED VALUES

To us mere mortals, the obvious has to be stated and restated, and even then we don't seem to comprehend. The biggest problem we have in this world is trying to get along. Nations with nations, religions with religions within those nations, and down to people with people. Those that seem to get along the best usually are those that have the most in common from where they were prior to being together, and they have evolved and espouse a synergistic set of goals for the future. When people can find themselves together with other people who share their feelings, and can work together in a mutual effort to accomplish their aspirations, you have accomplished something special. In a nutshell, that's what shared values are all about — working with people from similar backgrounds in an environment that's conducive to fulfilling everyone's goals.

It is also quite a task to get such a homogeneous group together at the right place, at the right time, for the right reason; but that's exactly what you are trying to accomplish by creating an excellent culture. That requires planning — strategic planning to get the team in position to make the transition from awful or fuzzy to excellent.

The Team Concept

Everybody in corporate America talks about the team and how important it is, but there are very few real teams. Every organization has a team on paper in their organization chart. However, my observations of most teams are that they are teams in name only, because each member is dancing to a different game plan, and when it comes time to play they fumble and then blame each other.

There is absolutely no way that you can have a good team without a good plan, and good players who understand the plan and have a desire to cooperate and support each other in the achievement of the organization's plan for the betterment of everyone. In organizations dominated by one person, or with a revolving door, or with a team recruited from every imaginable background, it is virtually impossible to have a good team.

Likewise, if the members of the team do not have personal career plans for themselves, they can't compare their plans for themselves against their organization's plan for them: if there is one. Without a plan it is very difficult for any team to be successful, and in turn, any person to be successful, but there are many firms and many people within them totally without a plan, working very hard.

How to Create Shared Values

The first step in the process of trying to create shared values is the development of a strategic plan and its by-product, the mission statement. If a firm, or a person, doesn't know what they want to be, it's obvious that they cannot be working towards any meaningful goal. They're probably trying to make themselves or the firm bigger or more profitable, or they're just trying to keep their jobs. With a good clear mission statement it is easier to see what products, at what share, in what markets, to what size are we working towards. In addition, it should also be made clear how we are going to do it (strategies) and what that represents in the form of a challenge. How we plan to treat our people, how we feel about our customers, the community, and the owners, should also be part of the plan, and written down.

What does this accomplish? It forces the team to agree on its purpose in being. It requires them to agree on what they are going to do now and why, and then what they are going to do in the future and why; and more importantly, which of them is going to do what to make it happen. It also should clearly stipulate what constitutes good performance and how that will be measured quantitatively, and what the rewards will be.

Once implemented, the plan has to be strictly monitored, with very specific periodic (at least quarterly) reviews of how are we doing against our short-term plans (the budget), how are we doing against our longer-term goals (strategic milestones), and what are we going to do about it if we are missing, or exceeding, one or both. Part of the plan development process should be the creation of well thought-out contingency plans with related trend indicators. These key performance indicators should be tracked more frequently (monthly) and flash reports prepared between periodic review meetings.

This process of planning, reviewing progress, and revising plans as a team really brings the team together and highlights the strengths and weaknesses of the team as well as the business. Over time, this interaction and series of successes and failures creates an environment with two very special and quite obvious characteristics:

1. Those that can plan well, and can make their plans happen with hard work and enthusiasm, stand out — as do those who cannot or don't seem to care, for whatever their reason.
2. A sharing, caring, cooperative and collaborative group emerges as the real team leading the organization into the future.

These characteristics are reflective of team building and the creation of goals with strategic significance for all the key players. It's very much like what gets to permeate winning sports teams, political teams, and military organizations that have created a common bond to win, an esprit de corps.

That is really what shared values are all about — getting the team together to rally around a long-range plan that they have developed; and if they can make it work it will be for the benefit and betterment of them all, their families and all of the other corporate constituents. Shared values are the embodiment and exercise of the total planning process by the key players who are ultimately and intimately wrapped-up in the process of exercising their career plans through their roles in the organization's plan. Instilling in the management team this desire not only to work together cooperatively, but openly to share the overall responsibility of managing without succumbing to the usual human selfish weaknesses, is a very special success.

How to Maintain Shared Values Through Good Management

When you study what perpetuates shared values in those organizations that have been able to sustain an excellent culture, it generally tends to be a total and absolute commitment to planning and management by system. It's a religious, almost ritual-like devotion to taking the precious time to worship the time-tested god of planning. In those firms where it has become a corporate way of life, they plan all the time, have indoctrination sessions for newcomers, and relate the entire performance appraisal system to establishing personal goals that are related, if even only in a small way for lower level employees, to achieving the overall corporate strategic plan. Part of these appraisal systems also has to do with working together cooperatively, being creative, and being a very definite member of the corporate family.

In many cases it's as if the company is prescribing a pattern and profile for the long-term success of every key player as it relates to the long-range growth and prosperity of the organization. In these kinds of organizations, employees, over time, start to talk about "quality of life" and "quality of product" as if they were one and the same. The creation and maintenance of shared values is truly the epitome of objective good management. When, through the efforts of genuinely devoted employees, you can place the importance of delivering a quality product to satisfied customers above chasing profits, you are building a very steady stream of future earnings.

These firms are constantly at the forefront of the product life cycle, and systematically move in and out of products and markets with smooth precision and what appears to be uncanny timing. However, it only reflects the implementation of strategies that were devised in prior planning periods being exercised in the present as but one step in the corporation's steady profitable walk into the future.

Appendix
The Plan for Planning
(A Recap of the Steps in the Process)

STEP	ACTIVITY	KEY ACTIVITIES
I.	Orientation:	a. What is planning? b. Why plan? c. What is "Strategic Planning"? d. What Strategic Management means. e. Terminology and Definitions.
	Who:	The Management Team — CEO, direct reports to the CEO, and other key employees.
	How Long:	One day.
	Where:	Offsite, preferably at a motel/hotel complex near the office.
	Assignment:	Each participant, including the CEO, fills out strengths and weaknesses worksheets. Should be done independently, objectively, and without consultation with the CEO.

Example: By Manager.

Strengths: _____

_____

_____

_____

Weaknesses: _____

_____

_____

_____

STEP	ACTIVITY	KEY ACTIVITIES

II.   Strengths and Weaknesses Review:

      a. Presentation of Strengths and Weaknesses by each member, with CEO's presentation last.

      b. Recorded by the Facilitator

      c. Objective discussion of each strength and weakness.

How Long: One day.

Objective: To reach consensus amongst the group as to what really are the strengths and weaknesses.

Assignment: All participants, including the CEO, should take their respective strengths and/or weaknesses and develop ways to make the strengths more and better, and improve the weaknesses, that is, to develop potential action plans (strategies).

Example: By Manager.

      Action Plan: What it is (potential strategy)

                      Rationale

III.   Potential Strategies Review:

      a. Presentation by each member of his potential action plan.

      b. Recorded by the Facilitator.

      c. Objective discussion about all of the proposed action plans to try to determine:

        1. Whether we can accomplish this with our existing resources (manpower and finances).

        2. Who will manage.

        3. Priority of action plans.

How Long: One to two days.

Objective: To prioritize action plans that the management team has the capacity to accomplish, by their agreed upon importance to the future of the business.

STEP	ACTIVITY	KEY ACTIVITIES

Assignment: For those that have been determined to be important, by respective manager (or in teams), work with subordinates to time-phase and cost-out each potential strategy.

Example:

Potential Strategies	Agreed upon as Necessary and Achievable
_____	_____
_____	_____

IV.   Cost-Out Time-Phase Review:

a. Presentation by all members of the results of their exercises.
b. Explanations of why some action plans were modified, some new plans created, and some aborted.
c. Reaction of subordinates to the process.

How Long: One to two days.

Objective: To arrive at a set of agreed upon strategies that have been well thought-through in the costing-out exercise, and time-phased in a way that can be accomplished while maintaining other operational responsibilities.

Assignment: For the CEO and planner — Step V.

V.   Mission/Strategic Plan

a. CEO writes the initial Mission Statement.
b. CEO, and/or planner, using the agreed upon strategies from Step IV, organize and complete the strategic plan document.
c. CEO assigns specific strategies to respective managers responsible for making them happen, and sets up a performance evaluation plan marrying compensation to strategic milestones.

How Long: CEO sets criteria.

STEP	ACTIVITY	KEY ACTIVITIES

      Objective: To get the Mission Statement written and the strategies organized into a document that can be shared with all of those employees, and others, that have a need to know.

      Assignment: Integrate the Strategic Plan with the Operating Plan.

VI.   Integration of Strategic Plan with Operating Plan:

         a. Planning guidelines memoranda.
         b. Strategies establish goals via quarterly milestones for operating plan horizons.
         c. Annual Budget developed from forecasts of base business and incremental business expected from effective implementation of strategies over the Operating Plan period.
         d. Operating Plan document prepared.

      Objective: To accomplish the ultimate purpose of the entire exercise: to have the Operating Plan driven by the Strategic Plan, with all of the prudent contingency plans.

STEP	OBJECTIVE	KEY ACTIVITIES

VII.   The Next Planning Cycle

         The next planning cycle is not a repeat of Steps I through VI, but rather, a review of the successes and failures of implementing strategies from the last Operating Plan. This review is compared with changes in markets and competitive strategies, and the strategic review process begins again.

Glossary of Strategic Planning Terms
(For the Uninitiated)

Annual Planning Cycle. Once-a-year event where progress against current strategies is assessed, markets and competitive positions are revaluated, and changes are made to operating plans to continue towards the overall goals of the strategic plan.

Assumptions (Planning). The results of analysis and trend indicators that provide the detailed tactical steps for strategies.

Base Business. The configuration of a company's products at the beginning of the planning process.

Budget(s) (ing). The month-by-month goals that have to be achieved to maintain an effective operating plan. The first year of the strategic plan. The quantification of plans for revenues and expenses for control purposes. The BEST estimate of next year's business.

Conceptual Thinking. The ability to look into the future and envision how the marketplace will be, and what products will be in demand in that future market. Also, being able to imagine how the company will have to be structured. A keen sensitivity to threats and opportunities.

Contingency Planning. Developing strategies to deal with what to do when what-if's become a reality. Thinking about and developing well-thought-out plans for favorable and unfavorable future circumstances. Planning for the orderly implementation of operational tactics to defuse crisis management.

Diversification Planning. What some companies use to describe their version of planning. It is usually an unsophisticated effort to "spread the risk," which, historically, has resulted in unnecessary, unprofitable, and ineffective acquisitions of products and/or companies.

Dynamics (Planning).   The constant nature of planning. The fact that the plan is never final. Markets are constantly changing.

Key Performance Indicators.   Generally, volume-related trend-determining data that is more an indicator of what will happen in the future than one of any historical significance, except for providing another period's worth of trend data. KPI's should be on the top of the management information list.

Long-Range Planning.   Generally considered an outdated, primarily financial exercise that extrapolates the present into the future using "wished-for" growth rates that are not based on any real planning assumptions. Planning by the numbers.

Milestones (Strategic).   Quarterly goals of individual strategies.

Management Information System.   The data that is compiled (either manually or via computer) and formatted for management review, and which gives the management team the key performance indicators to assess the future, and the budget-to-actual comparisons to control the present. Most of this information makes up the monthly manager's report.

Management System.   Another way of referring to Strategic Planning.

Mission Statement.   Management's clear explanation of what business or businesses the company is in now and why, and then how the management team plans to manage the future in terms of products, markets, and competitive positioning.

Operating Plan.   The first three years of the strategic plan, of which the first year is the budget. When complete, the operating plan should enable any reader to have a good understanding of the near-term future direction of the business.

Organizational Climate.   How everybody feels about what they are doing. Strategic Planning requires a climate that is conducive to planning – not a negative, secretive, or disconcerted one due to poor communication about planning. The product of the corporate culture.

Planning.   Thinking about how the business is going to be over the next three to five years in terms of how the markets, competitors, and technology may change. Developing a process to guide the company from where it is to where management would like it to be. An integral part of managing.

Portfolio Analysis.   Breaking all of the company's products down into a relationship between the share of a given market and the growth status of that market. Then assigning a management time and effort value to each product. An input to strategic planning and strategic management.

Quarterly Review.   Opportunity to review budget-to-actual for budget year, and strategic milestones and their related capital expenditures. It is an opportunity for management to reallocate resources based upon the to-date success or failure of individual strategies.

Strategy.   A well-thought-out, time-phased, and costed-out plan to effect a significant change in some aspect of business direction. An agreed-upon sense of direction for the management team. Part of the overall mission.

Strategic Planning.   A systematic and continuous disciplined approach to analyzing trend indicators about markets, competitors strategies, and your own product mix. Should engender a mission statement to set parameters on future growth, and detail individual strategies to make that growth happen. A system for managing better.

Strengths.   Those things, in the opinion of the management team, that should be capitalized upon and made better as strategies, or be put to better use, operationally.

Tactics.   The individual time-phased steps in a strategy.

Team (Management).   Usually the CEO and the direct reports to the CEO, but can be expanded to include other key employees.

Weaknesses.   Those things, in the opinion of the management team, that need to be improved or eliminated, and for which strategies have to be developed or operationally changed, quickly.

What-if.   A generally accepted modeling concept that takes potential business situations (what if this were to happen) and attempts to develop contingency plans to deal with them. A way of creating a wide range of possible futures, on paper.

Index